You're about to embark on a journey across the world and meet creatures and deities beyond your imagination.

For this year, instead of partaking in the usual Inktober, I decided to create a prompt of my own that featured various mythological figures of my choice. For this prompt, I broke it out into 4 weeks with each week having a different category. The categories I chose were Egyptian, Greek, Japanese and Norse. Within those categories, I picked my favorite deities and other mythological figures and creatures depicted in my own unique way. These drawings were also done with pen and ink and gold leafing pen.

In my research for putting this list together, I discovered a lot of interesting mythological figures and creatures that I didn't know of and was very excited to take what I learned and put my take on it. I didn't put in descriptions for the ones I did, but I highly encourage you to research these on your own if you find ones throughout this book that are interesting to you.

The ancient world is a fascinating place...

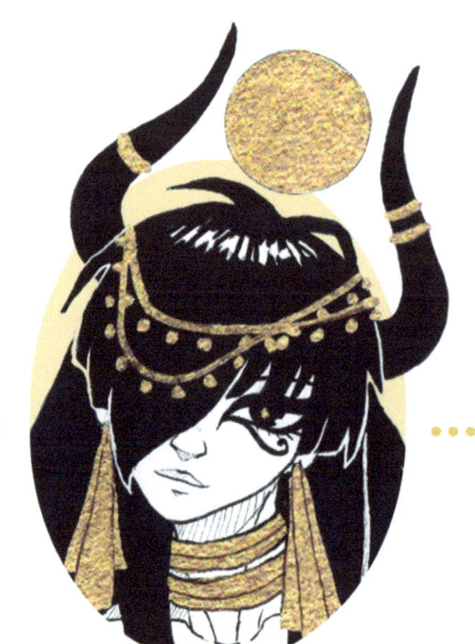

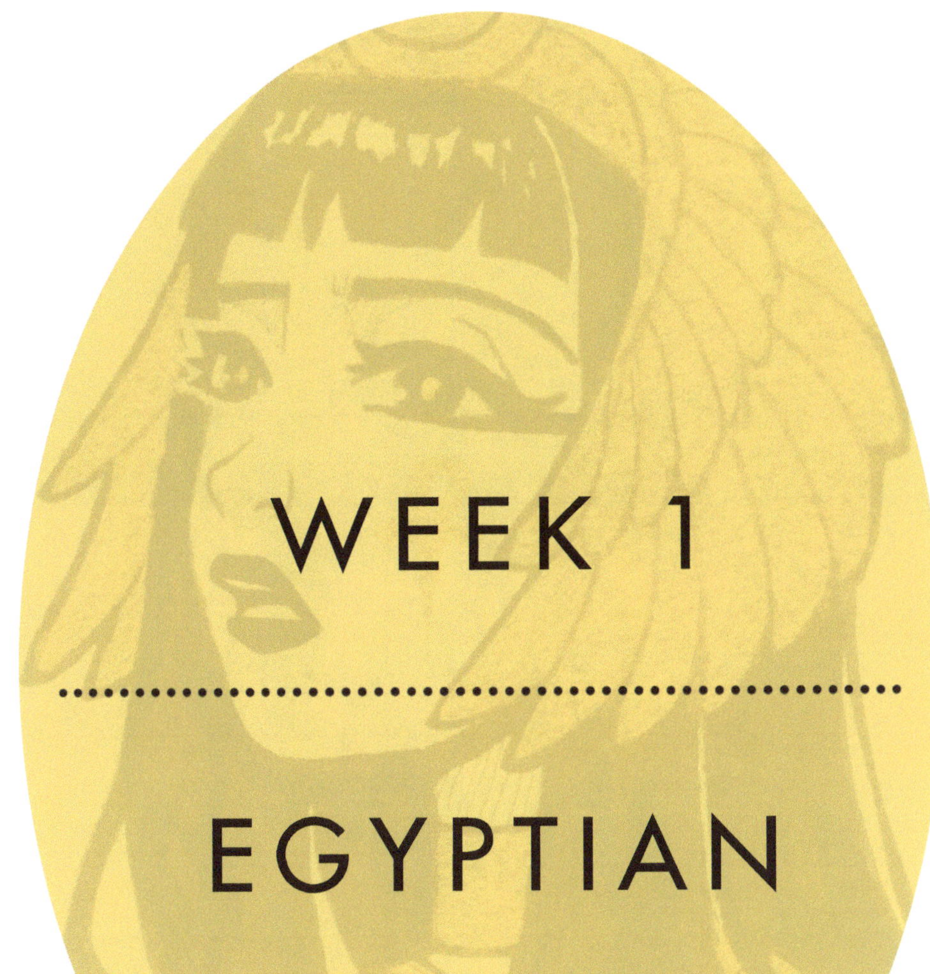

WEEK 1

EGYPTIAN

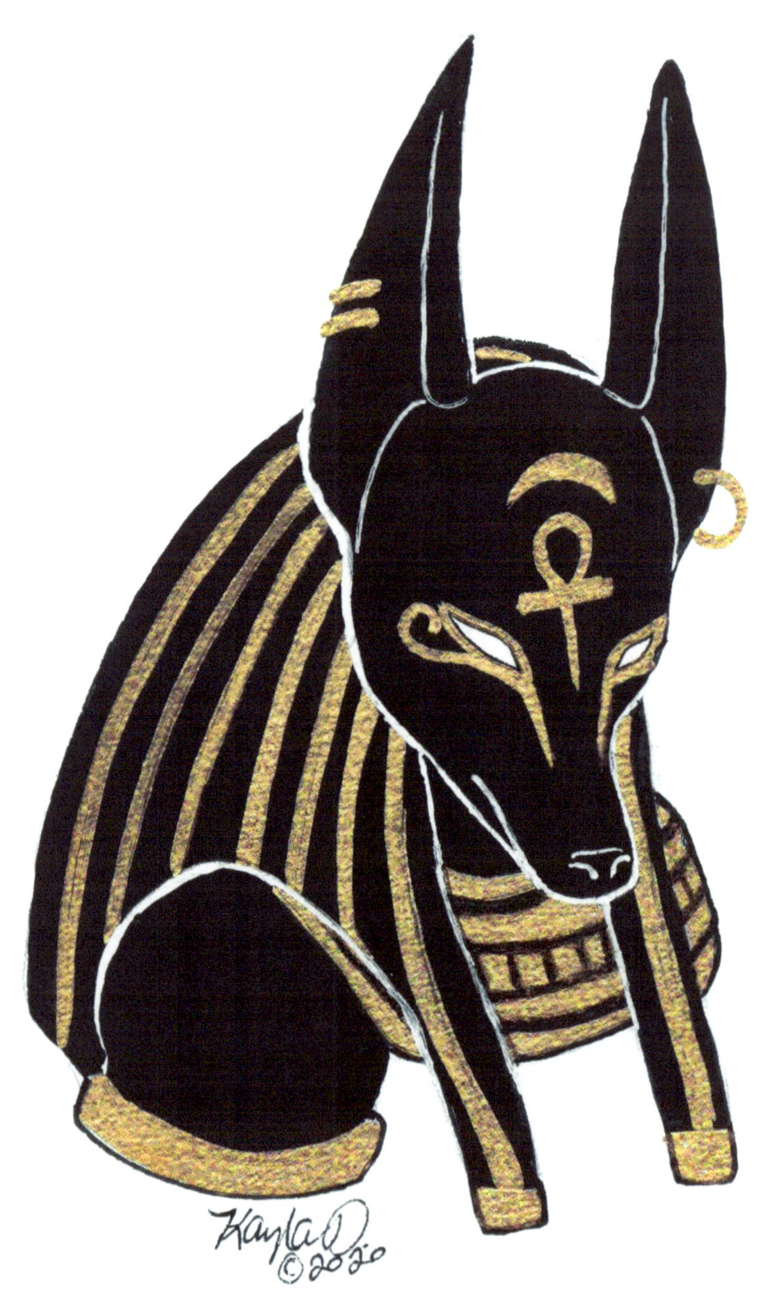

DAY 1 - ANUBIS

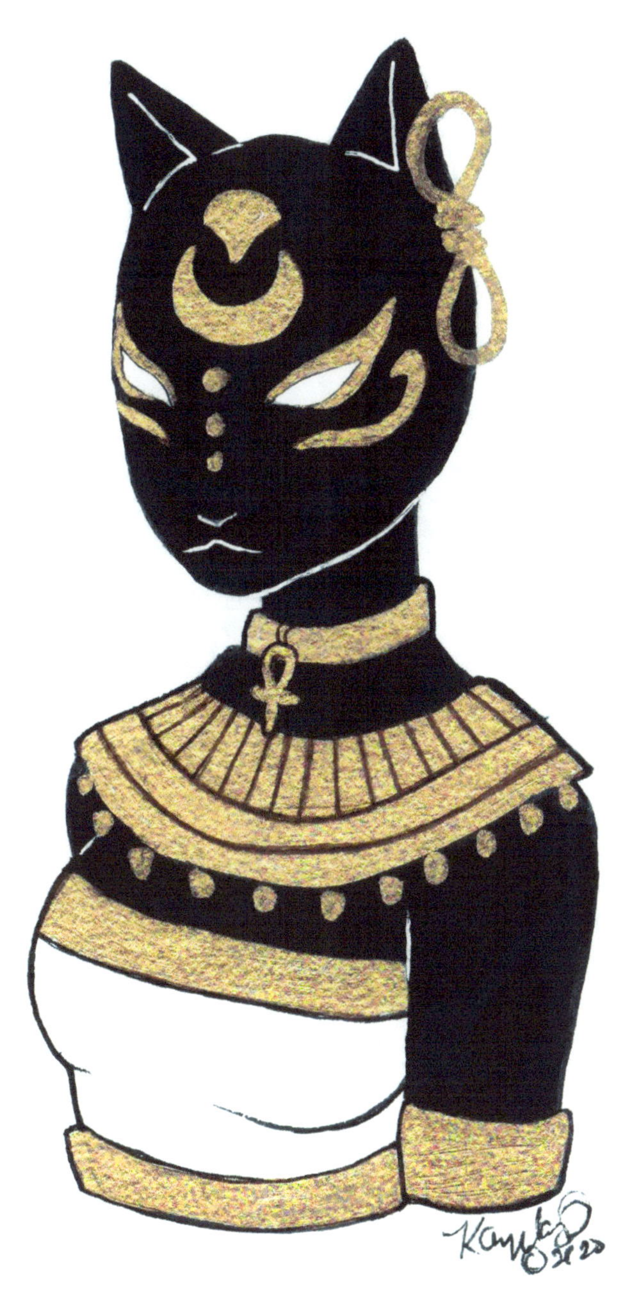

DAY 2 - BASTET

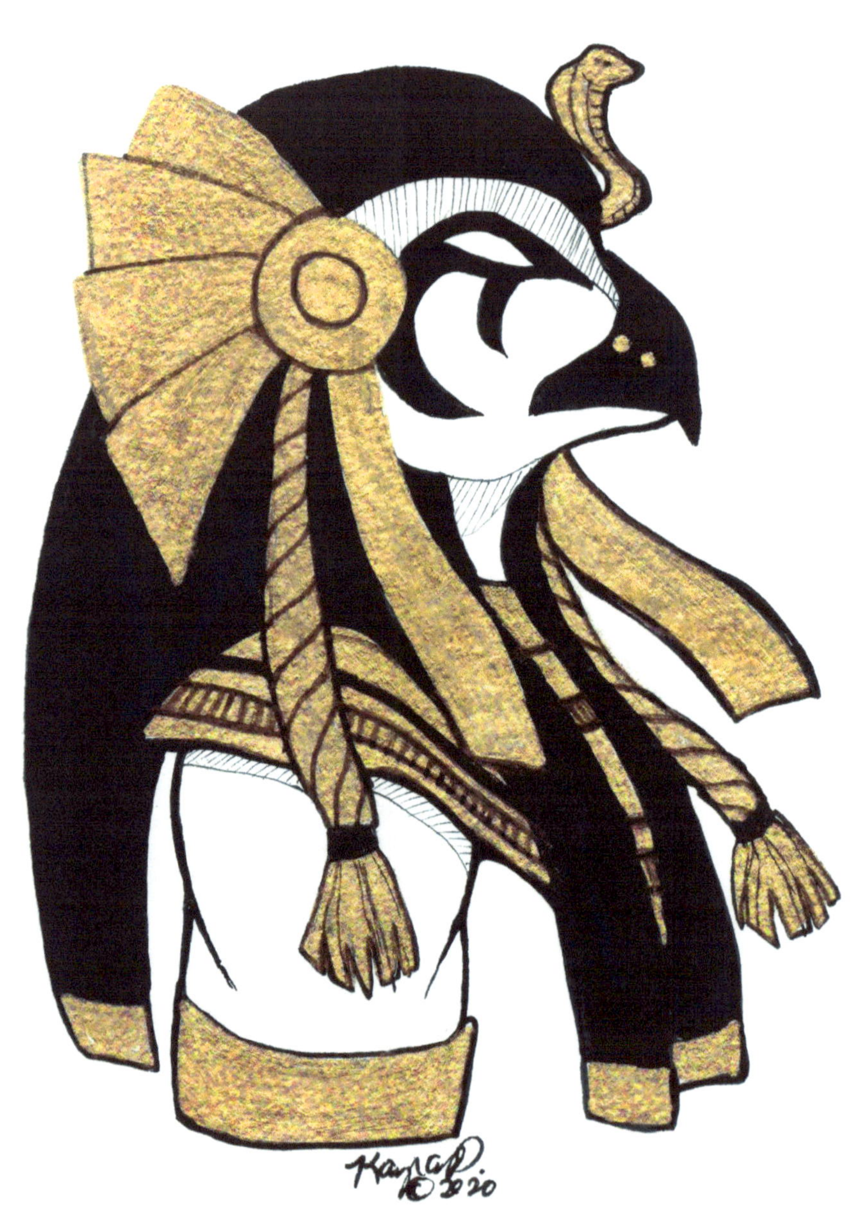

DAY 3 - HORUS

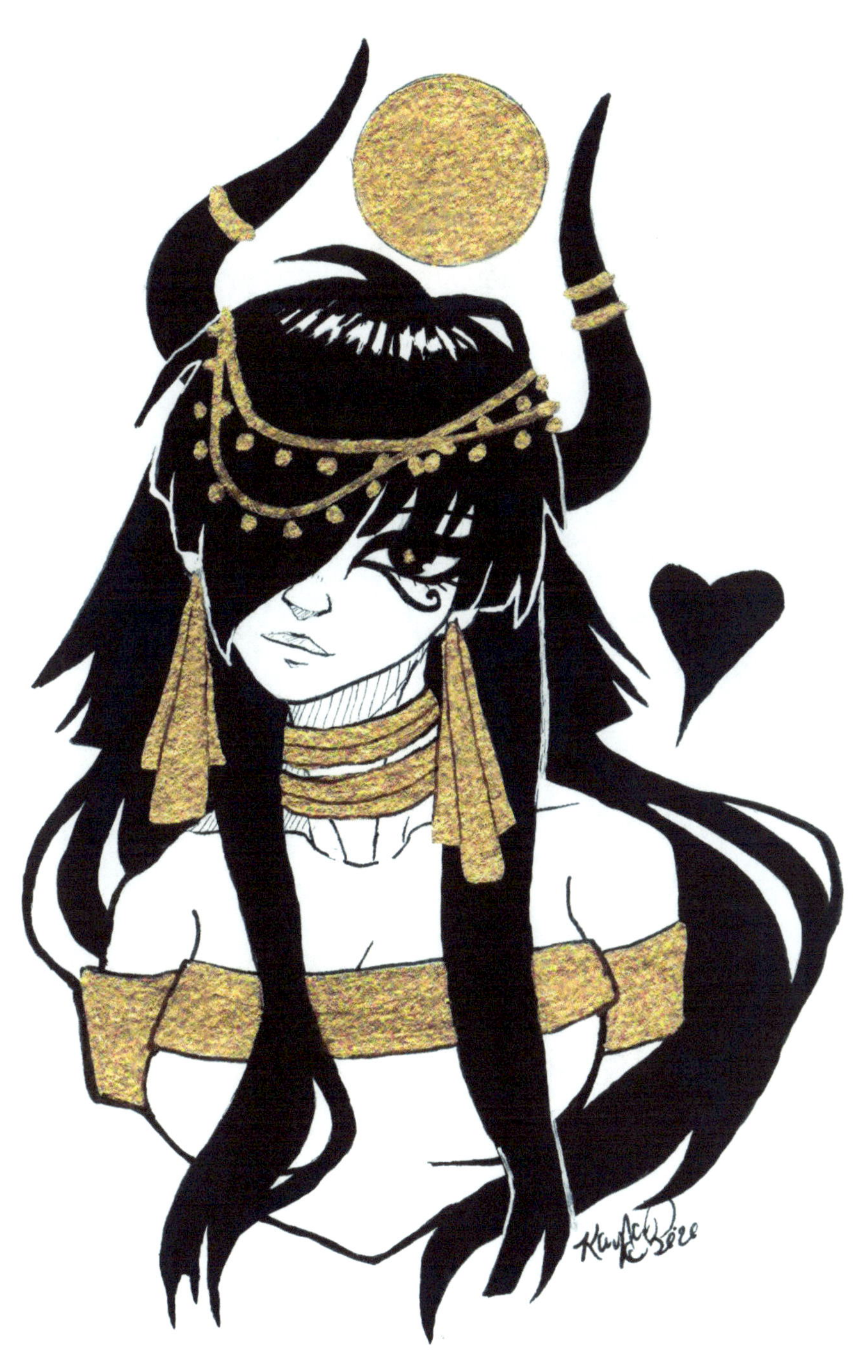

DAY 4 - HATHOR

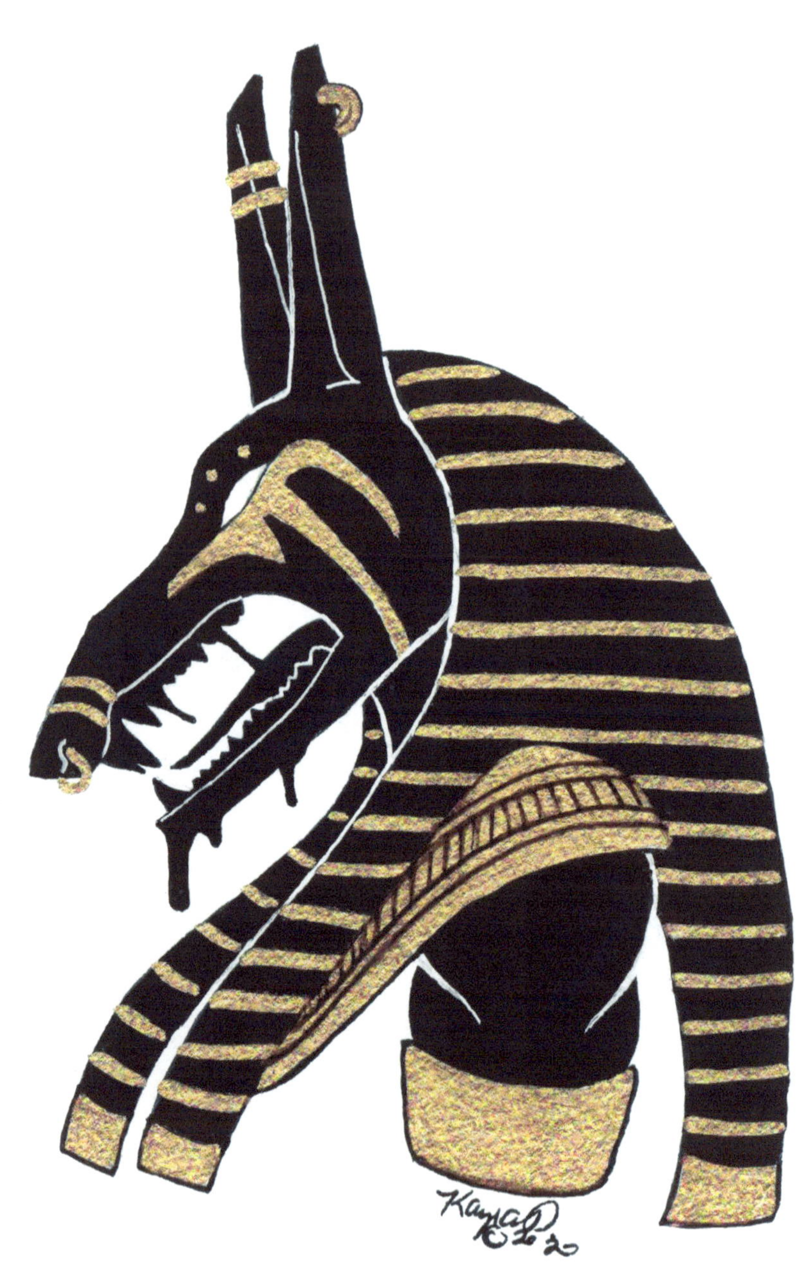

DAY 5 - SET

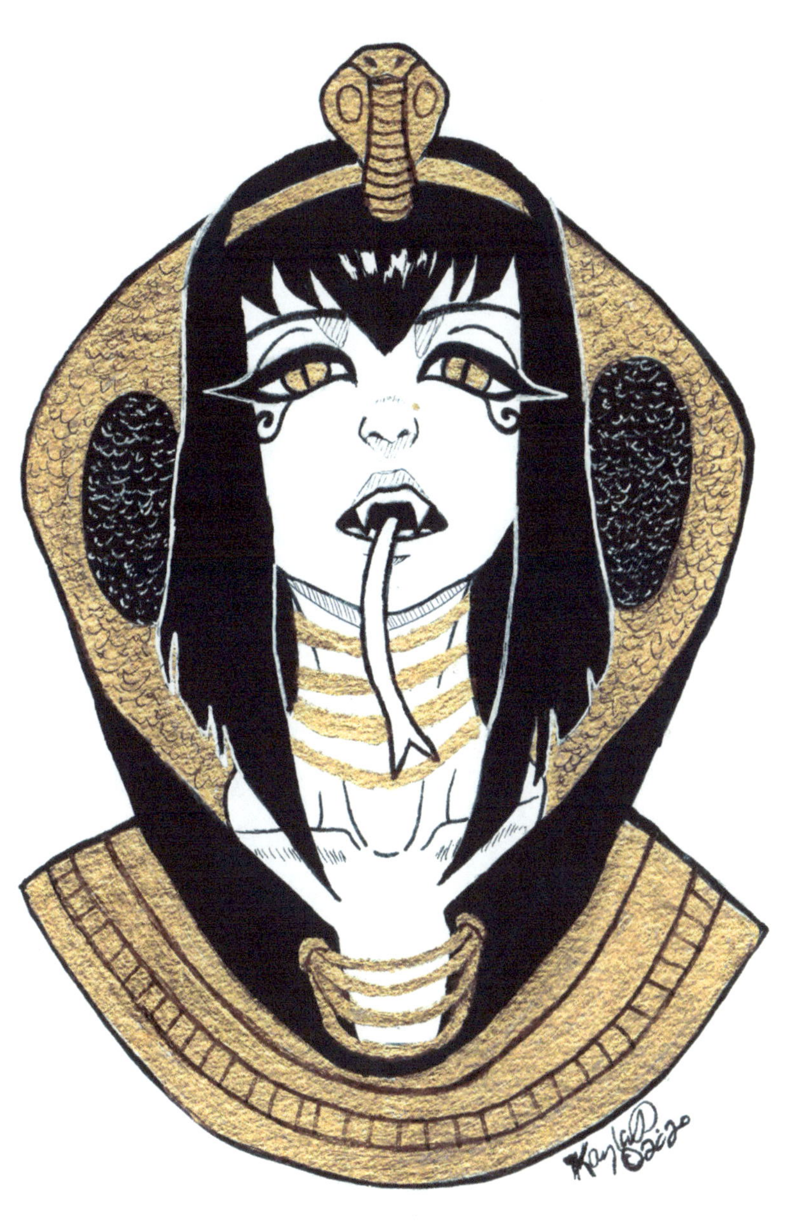

DAY 6 - WADJET

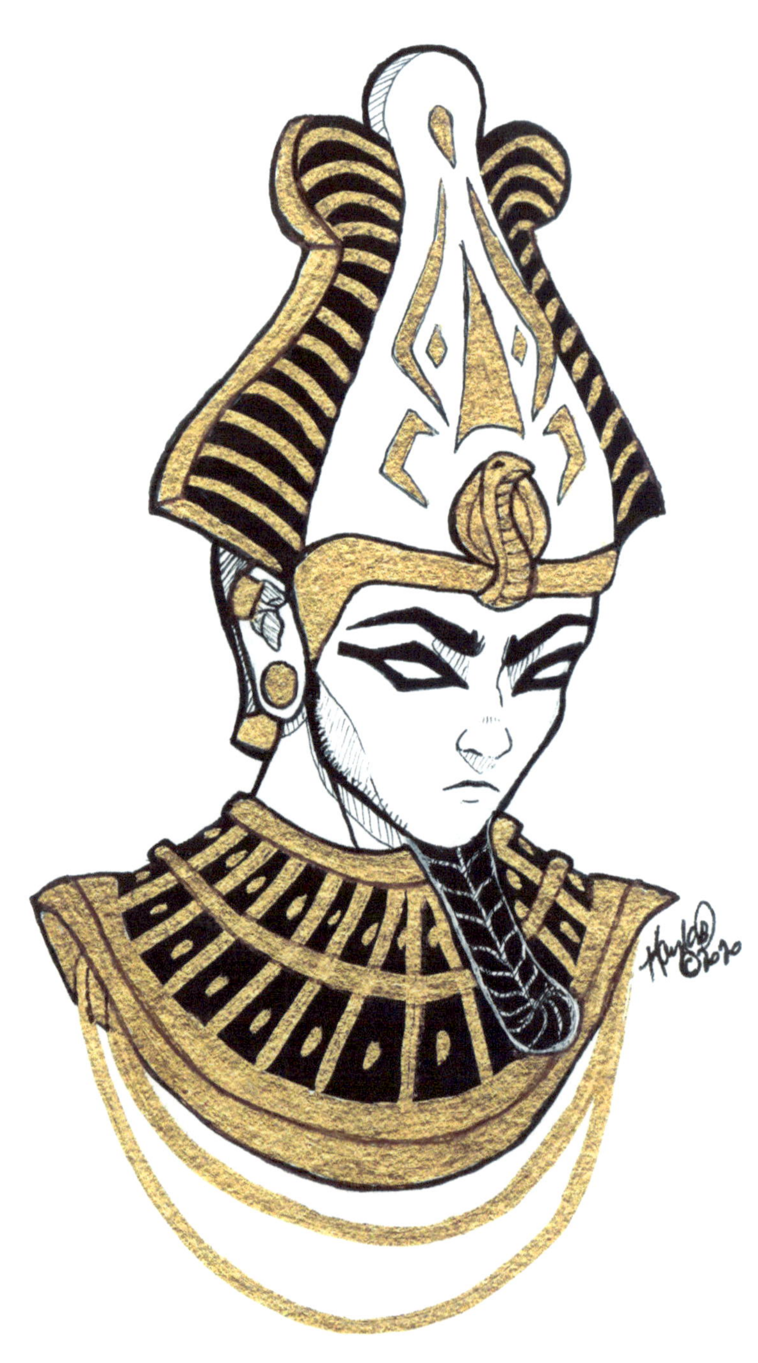

DAY 7 - OSIRIS

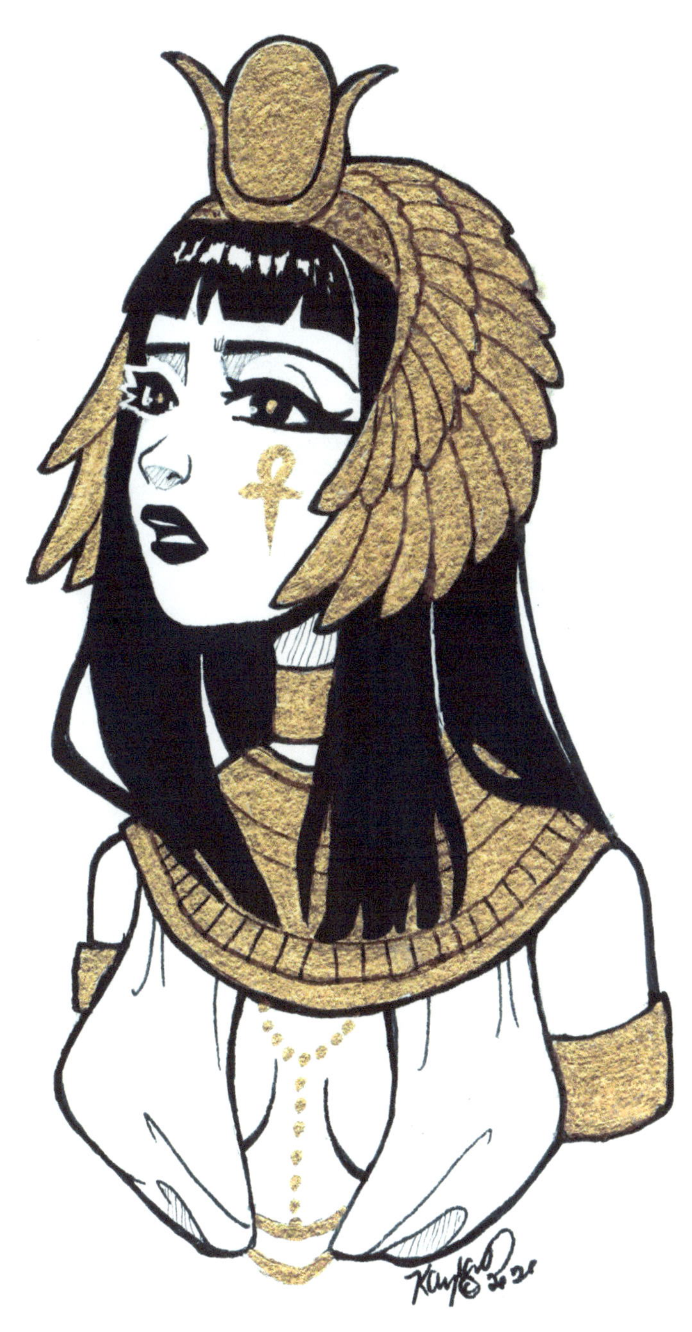

DAY 8 - ISIS

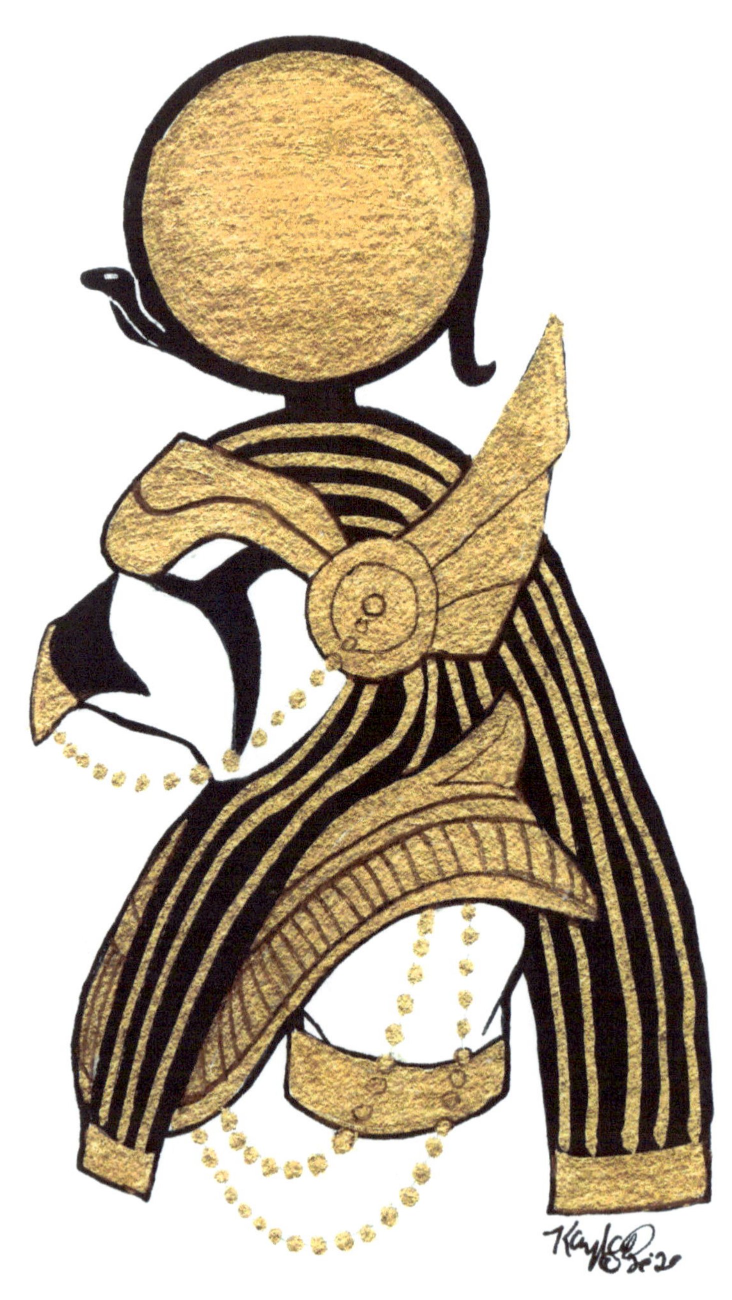

DAY 9 - RA

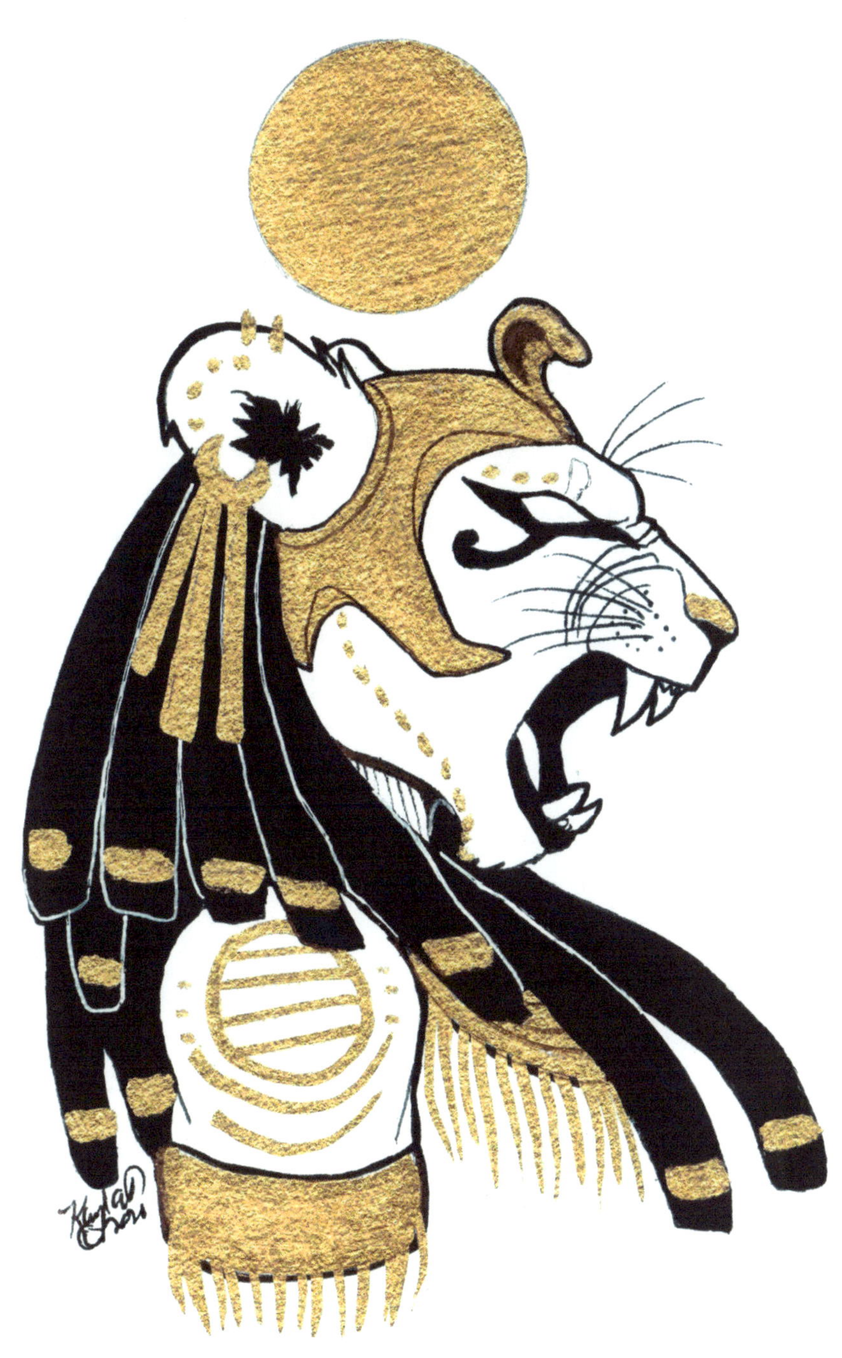

DAY 10 - SEKHMET

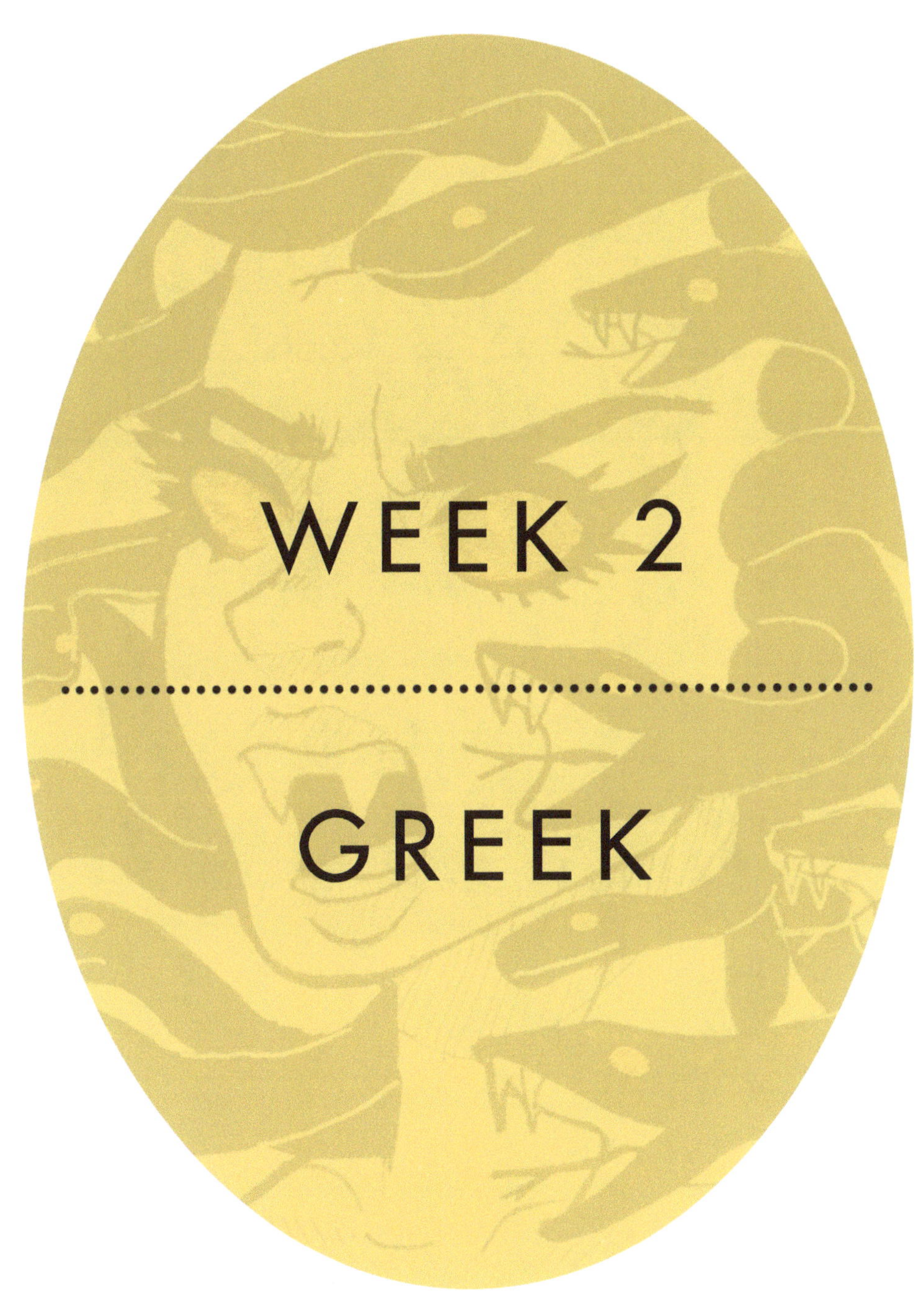

WEEK 2

GREEK

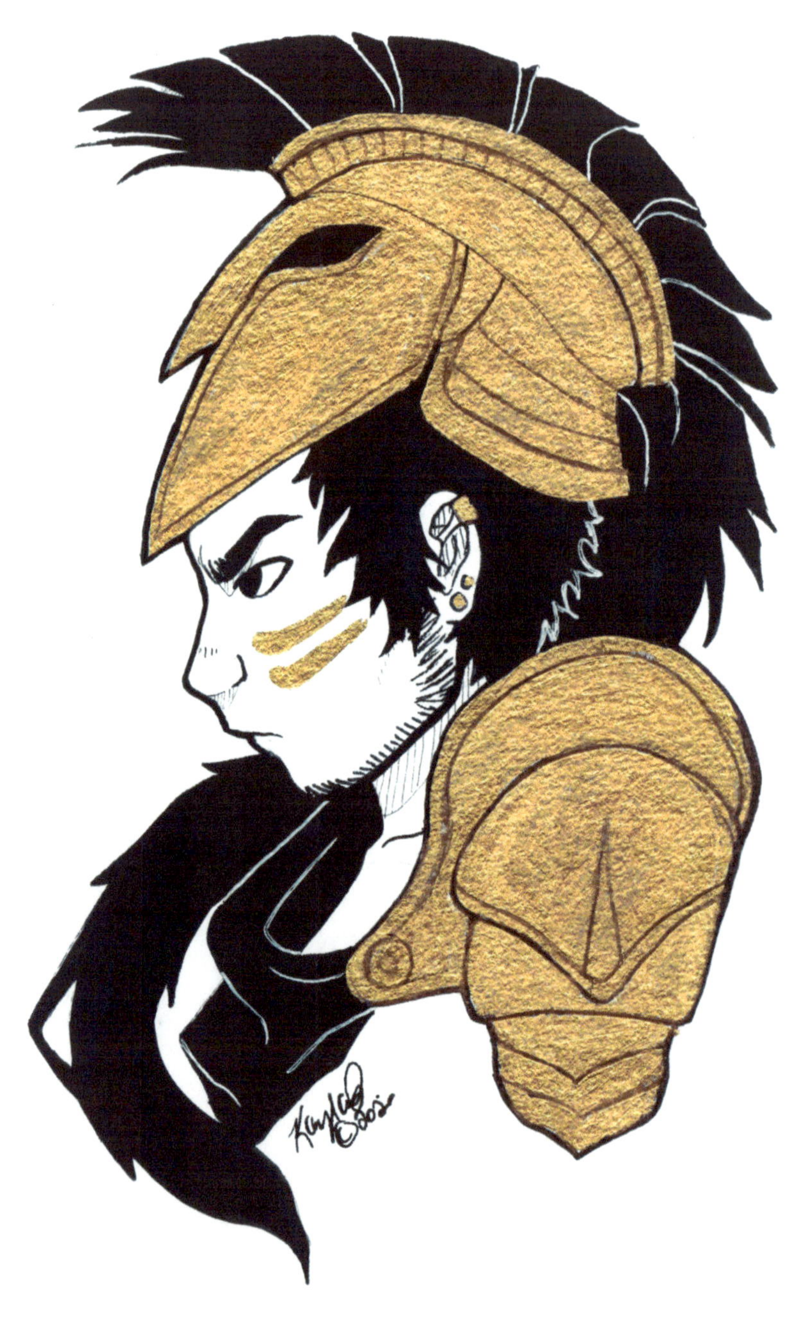

DAY 11 - ARES

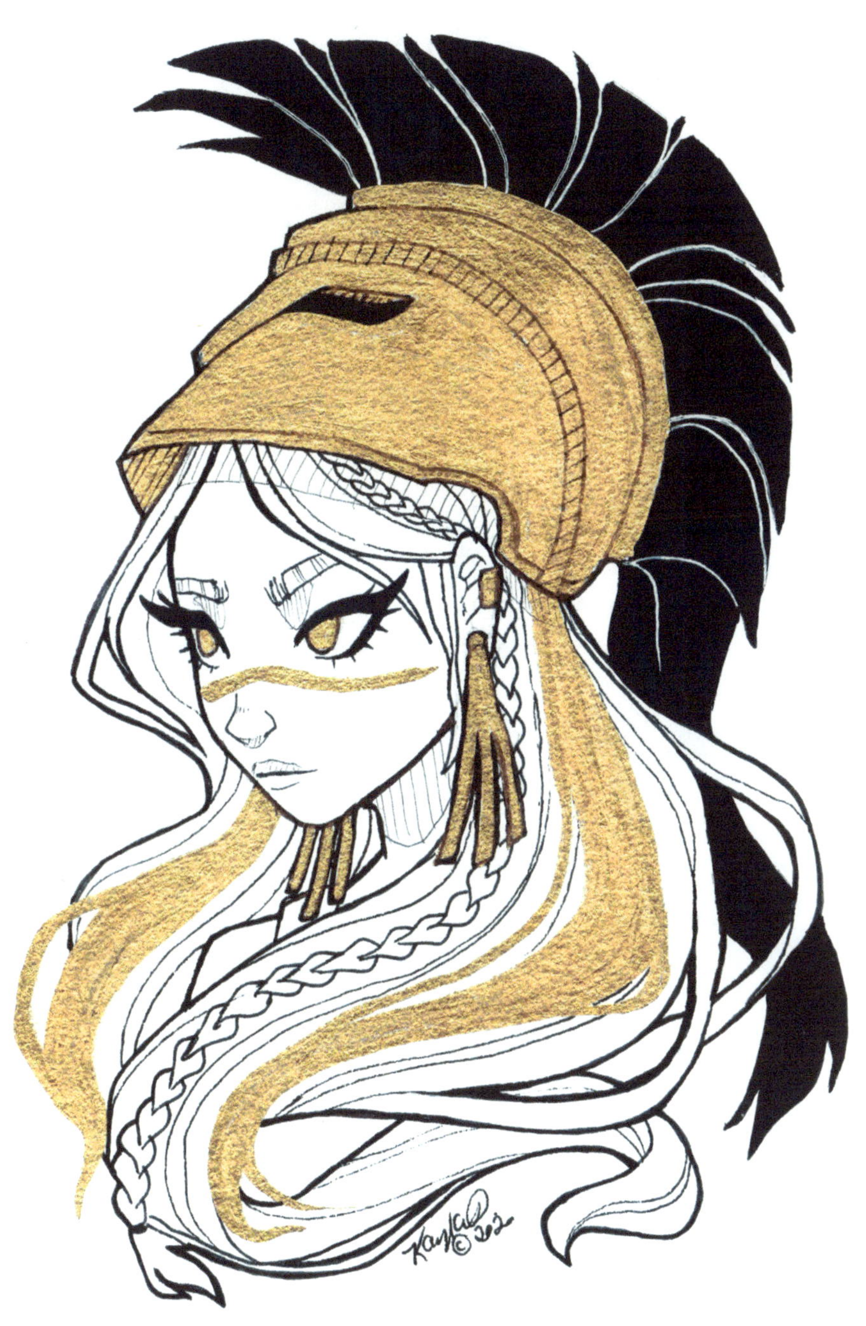

DAY 12 - ATHENA

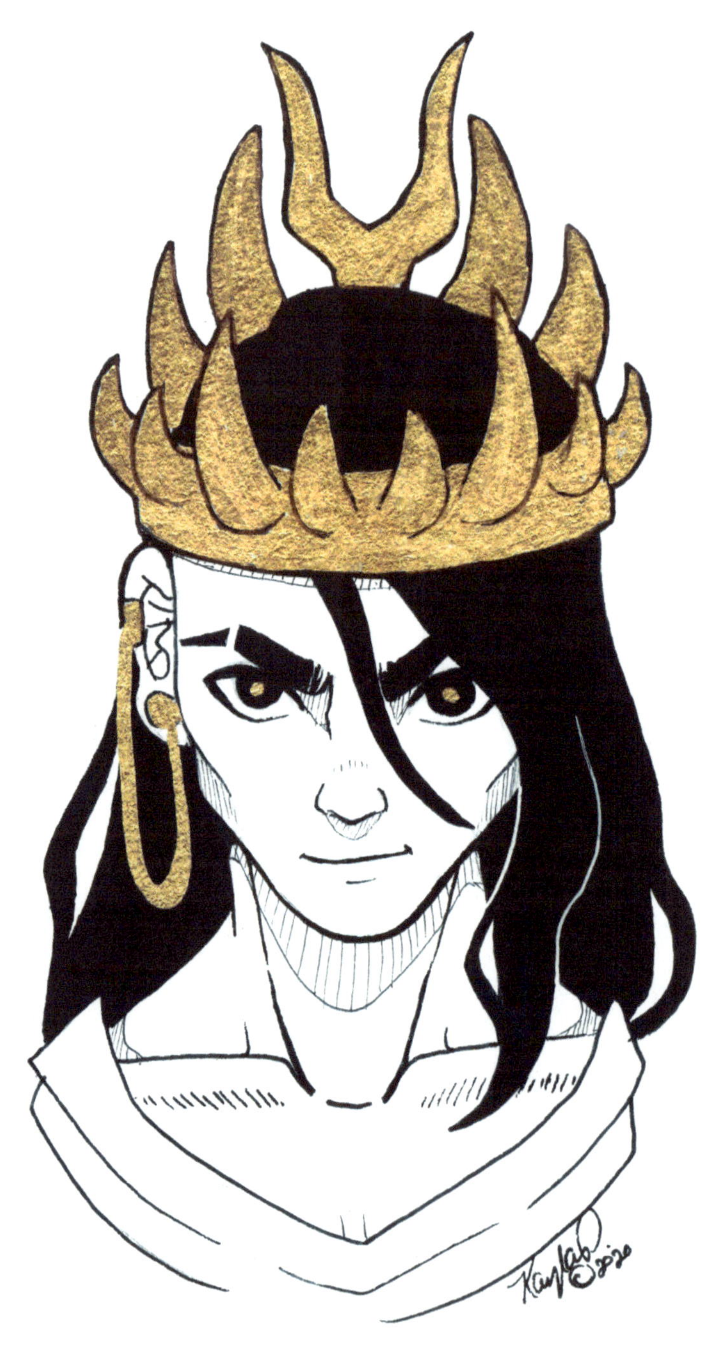

DAY 13 - HADES

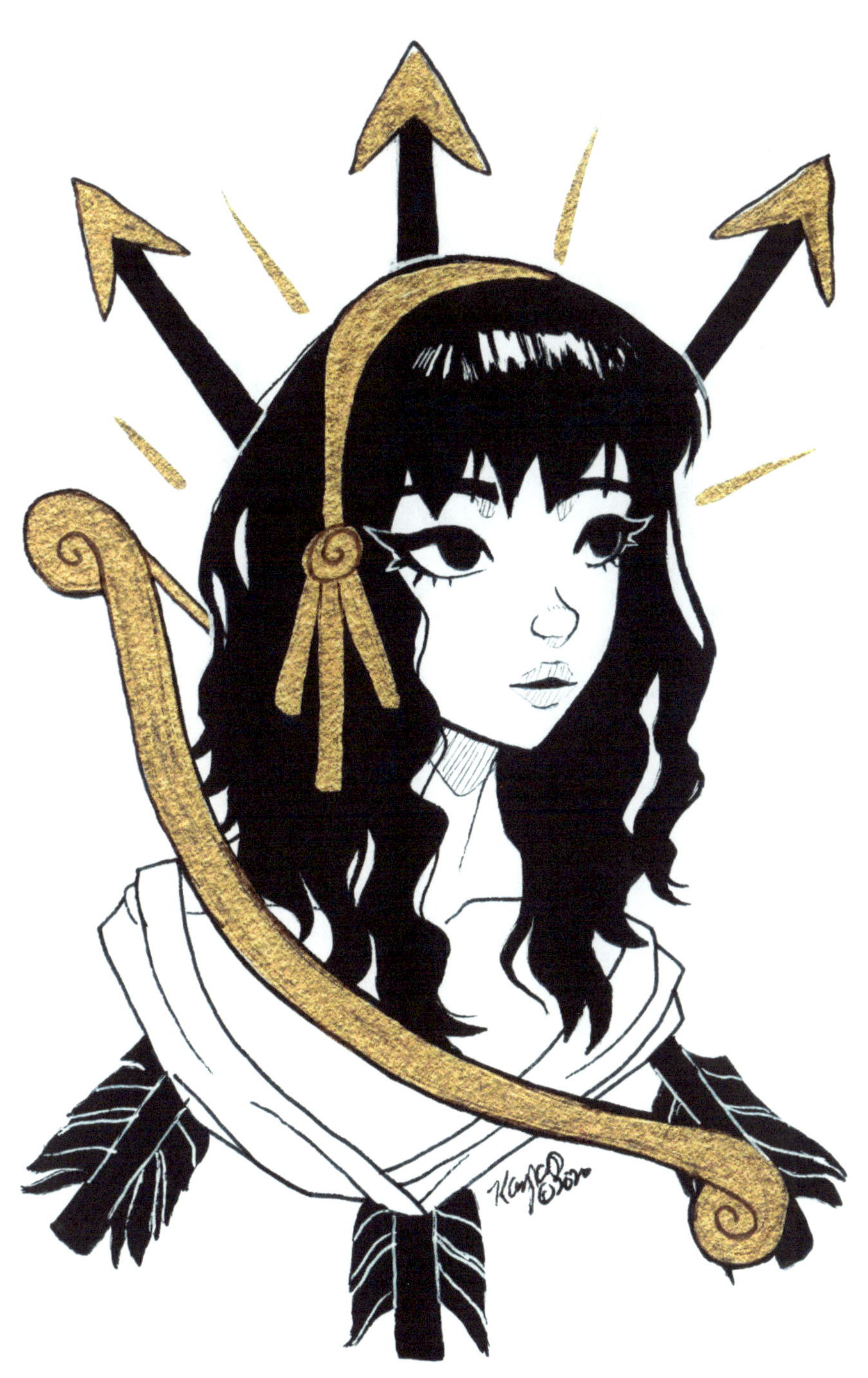

DAY 14 - ARTEMIS

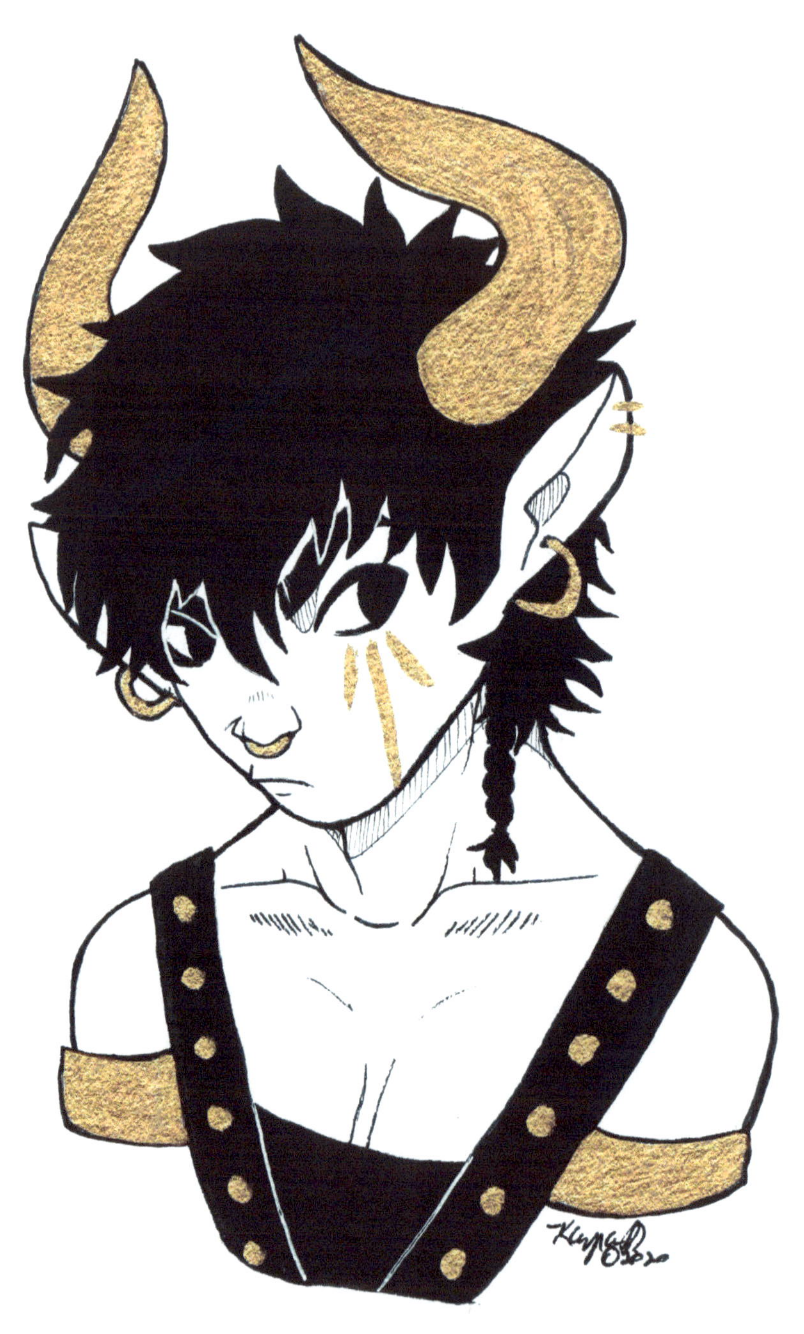

DAY 15 - MINOTAUR

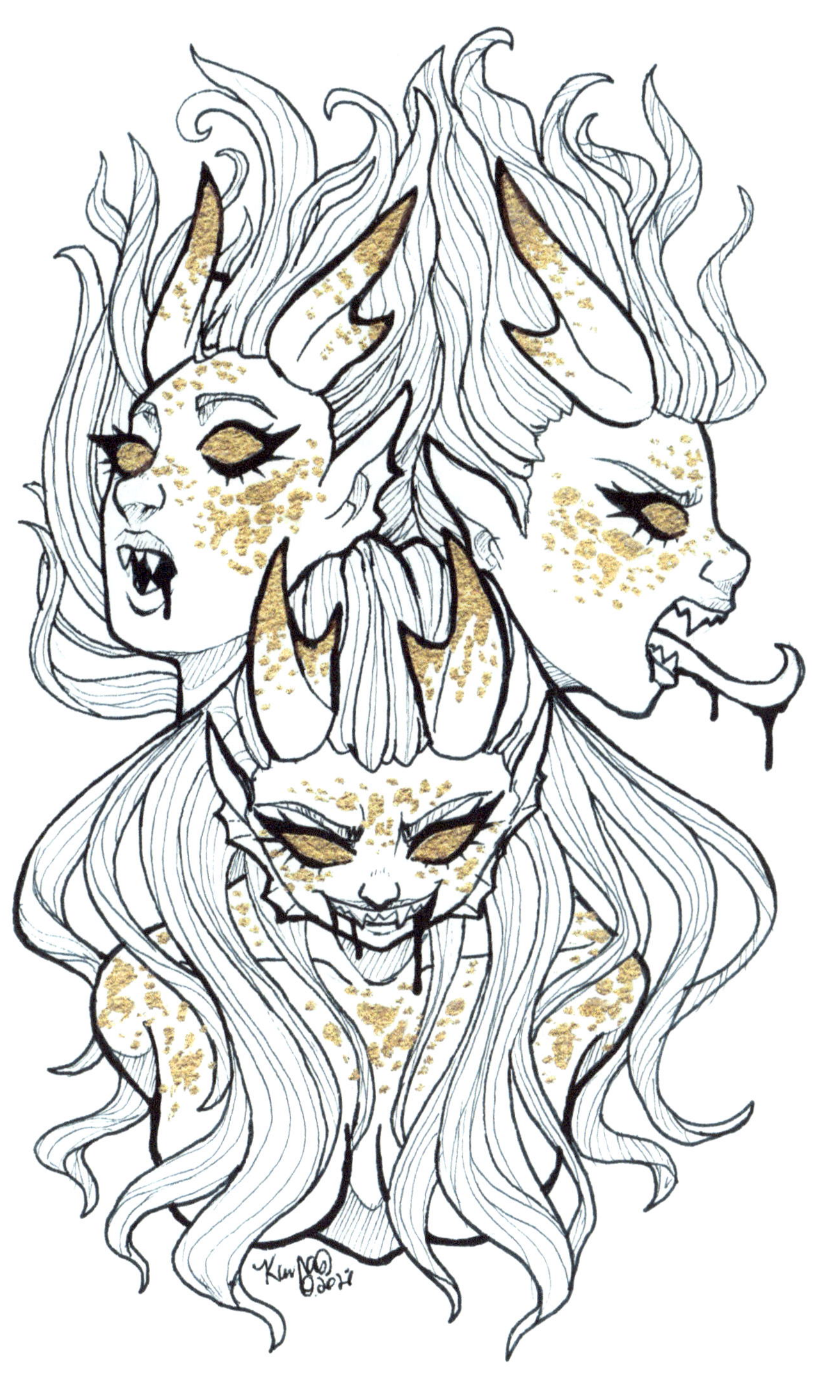

DAY 16 - HYDRA

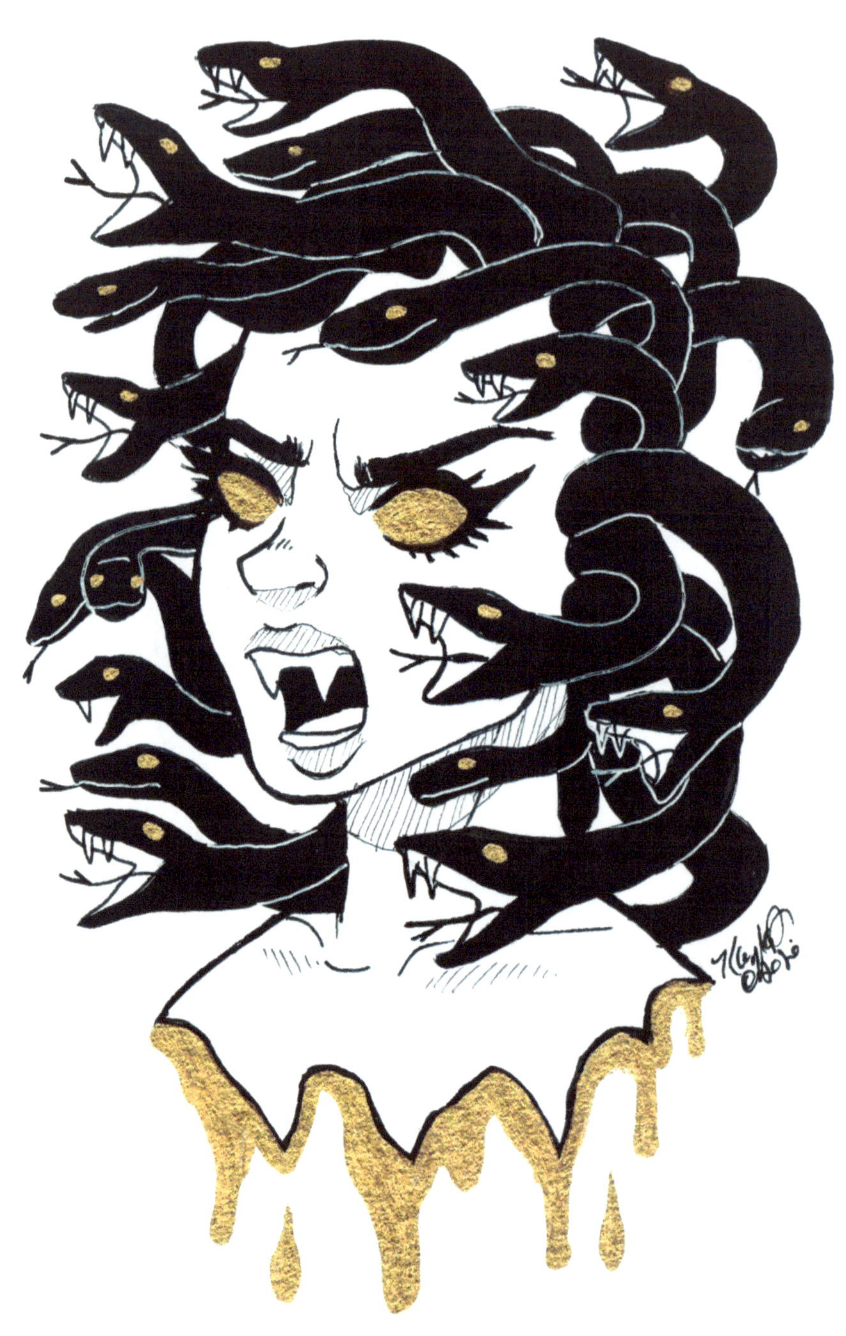

DAY 17 - MEDUSA

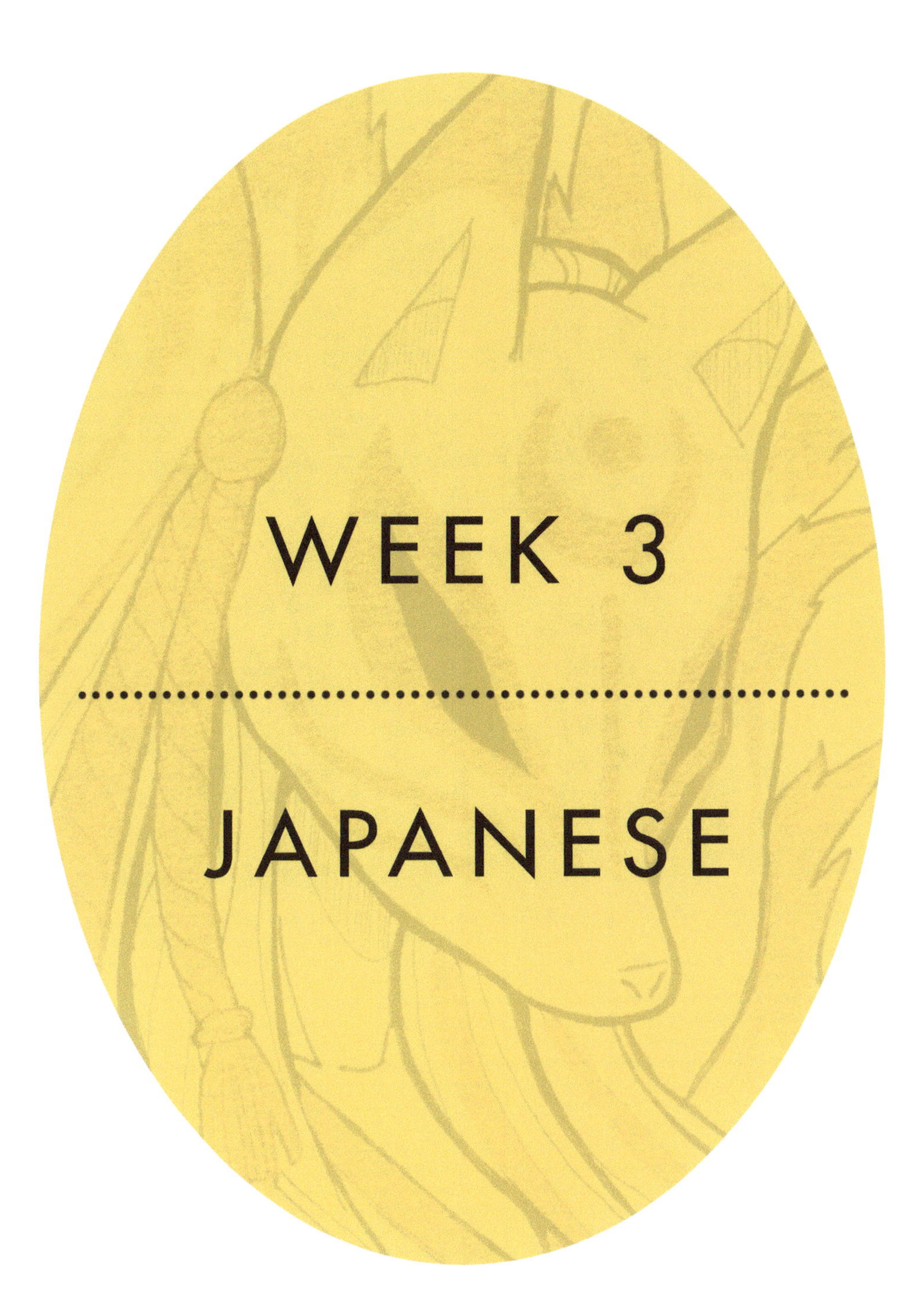

WEEK 3

JAPANESE

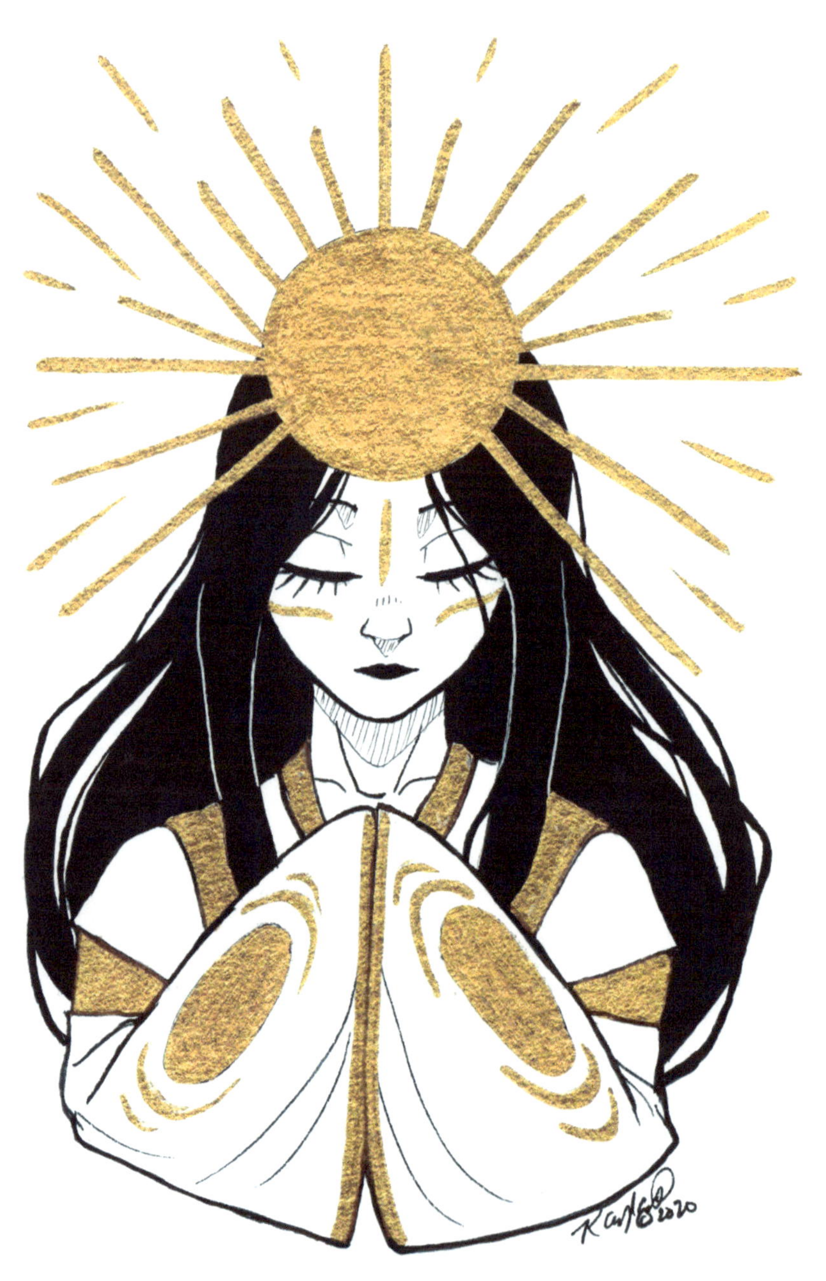

DAY 18 - AMATERASU

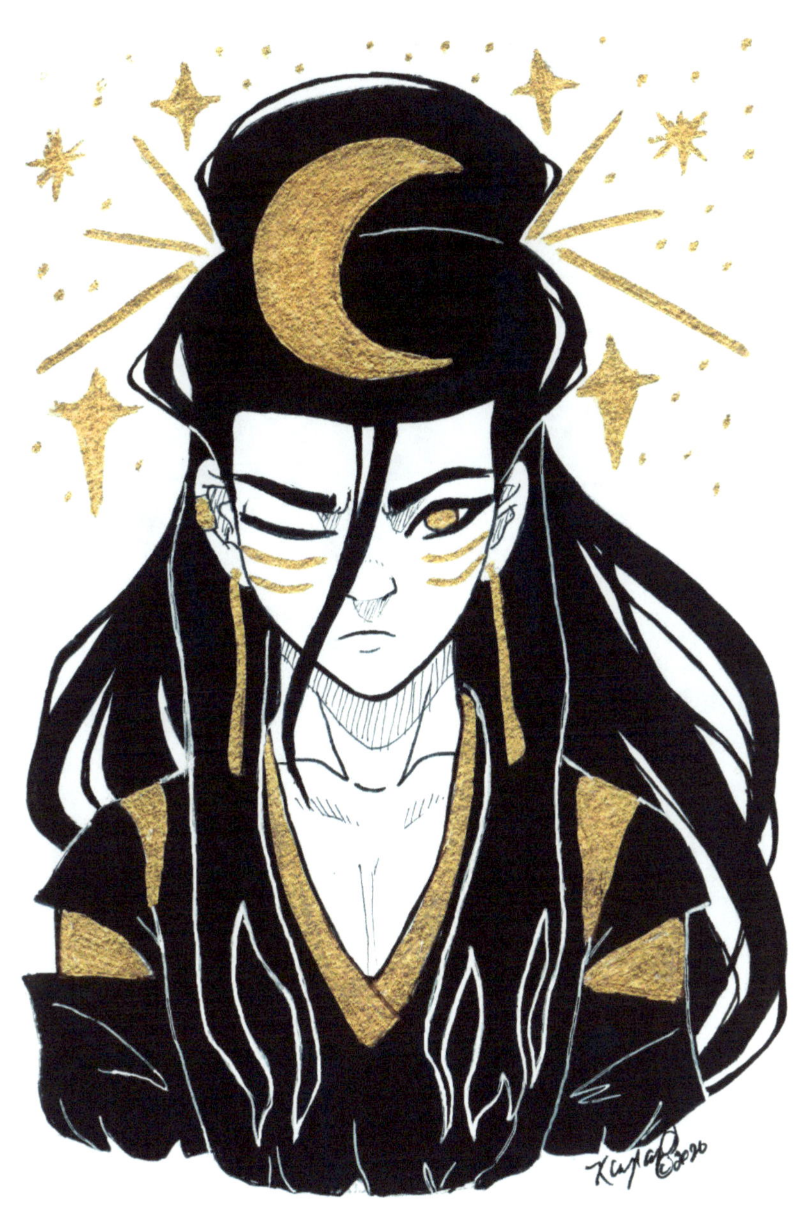

DAY 19 - TSUKUYOMI

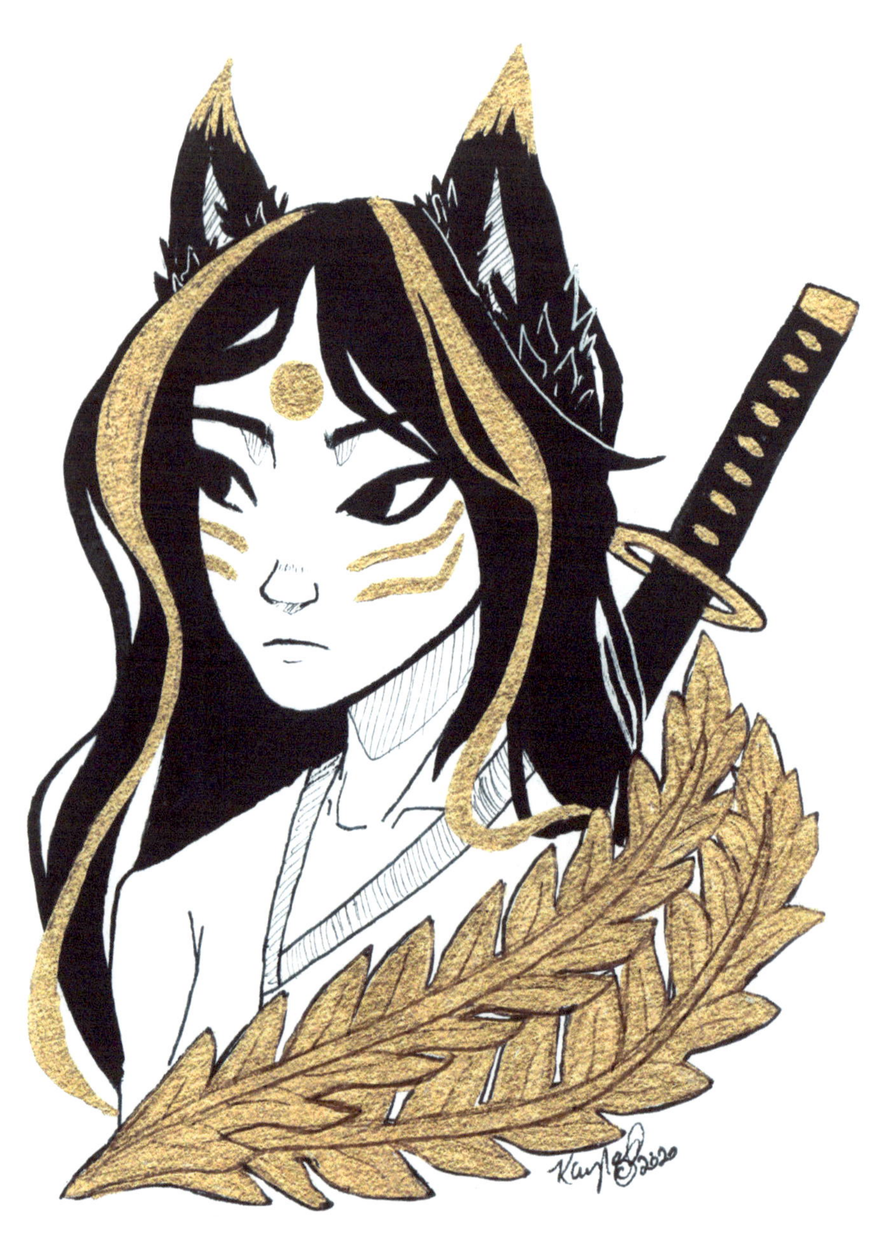

DAY 20 - INARI

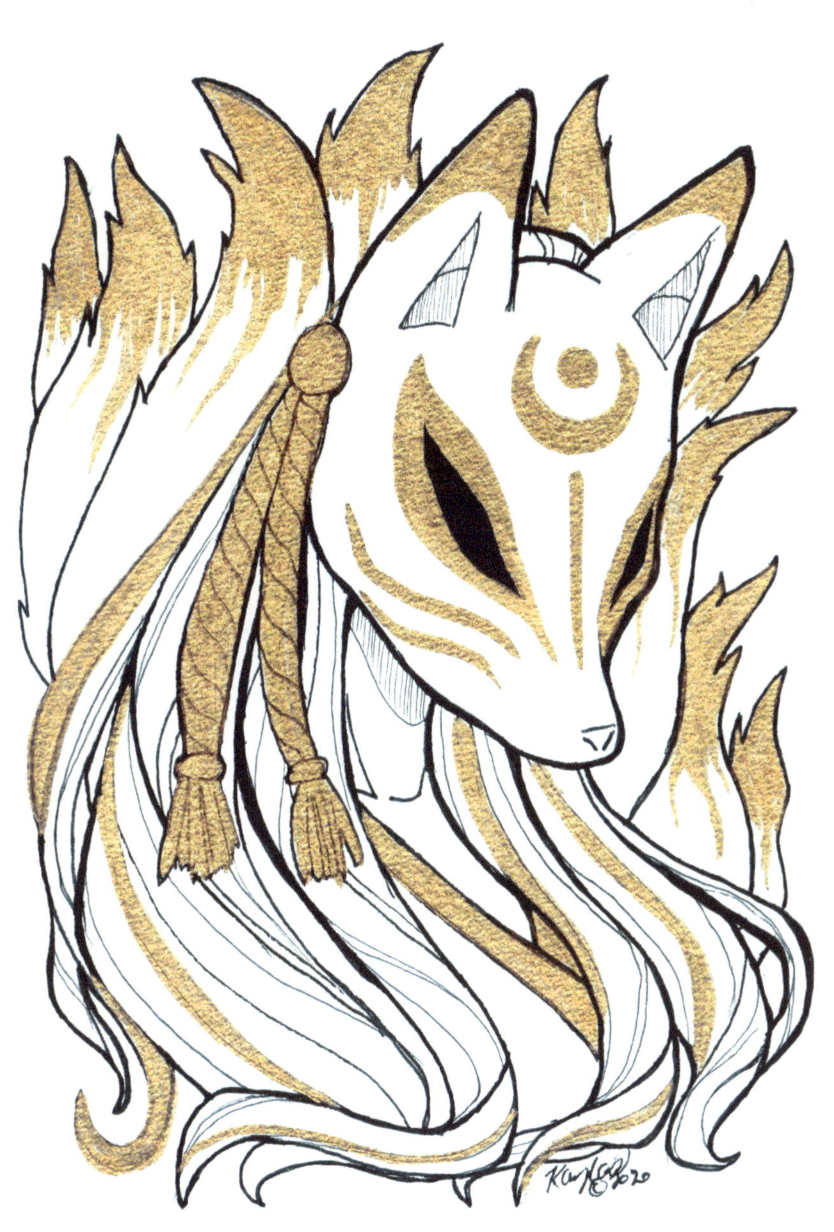

DAY 21 - KITSUNE

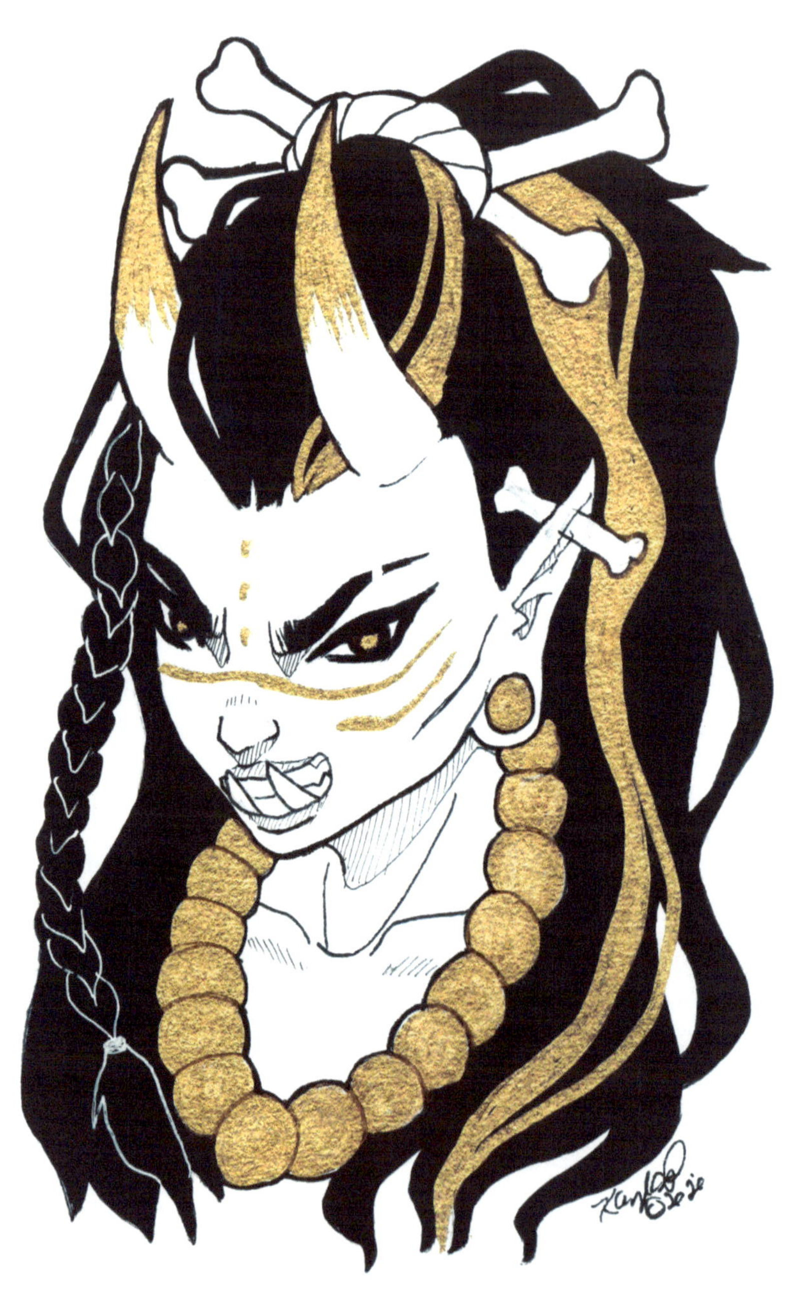

DAY 22 - ONI

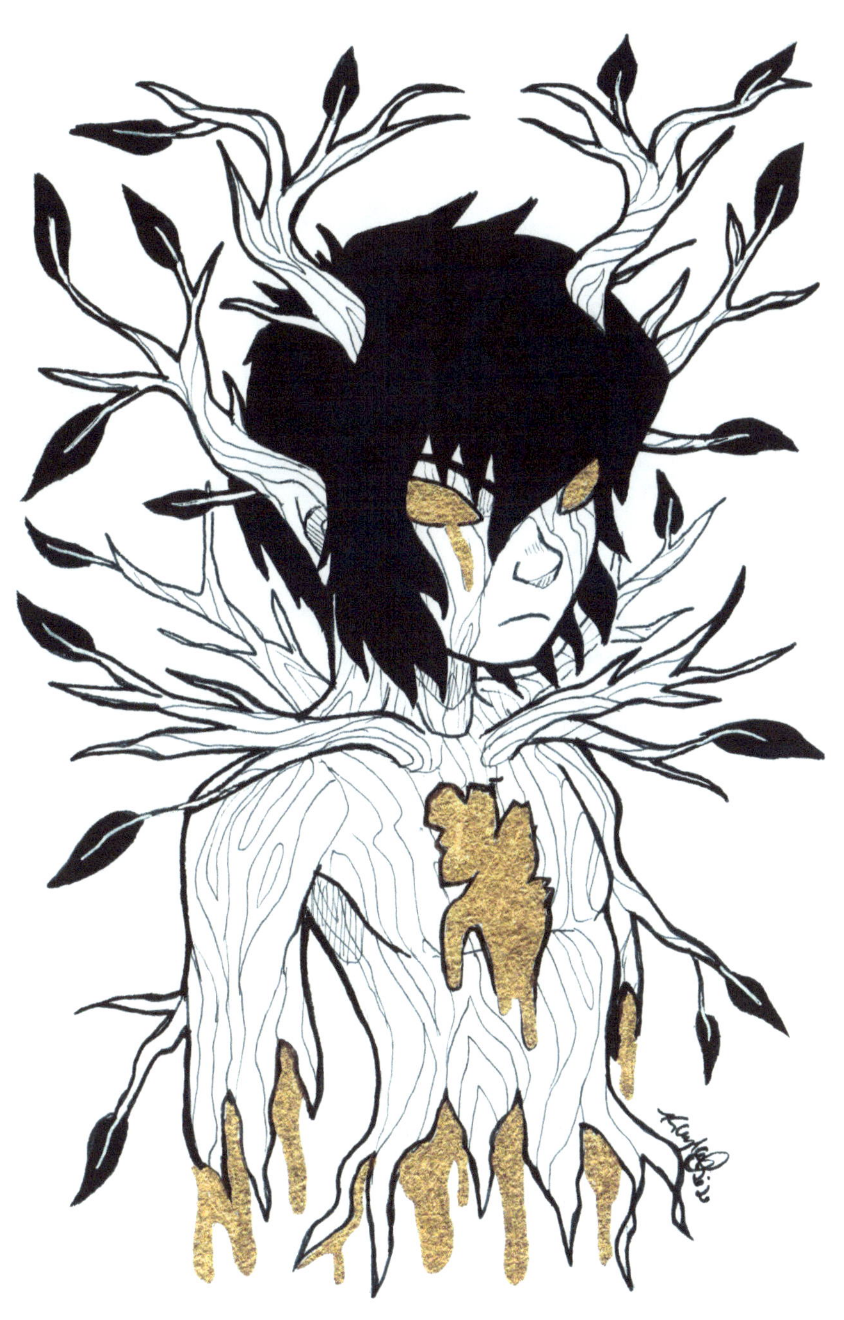

DAY 23 - JUBOKKO

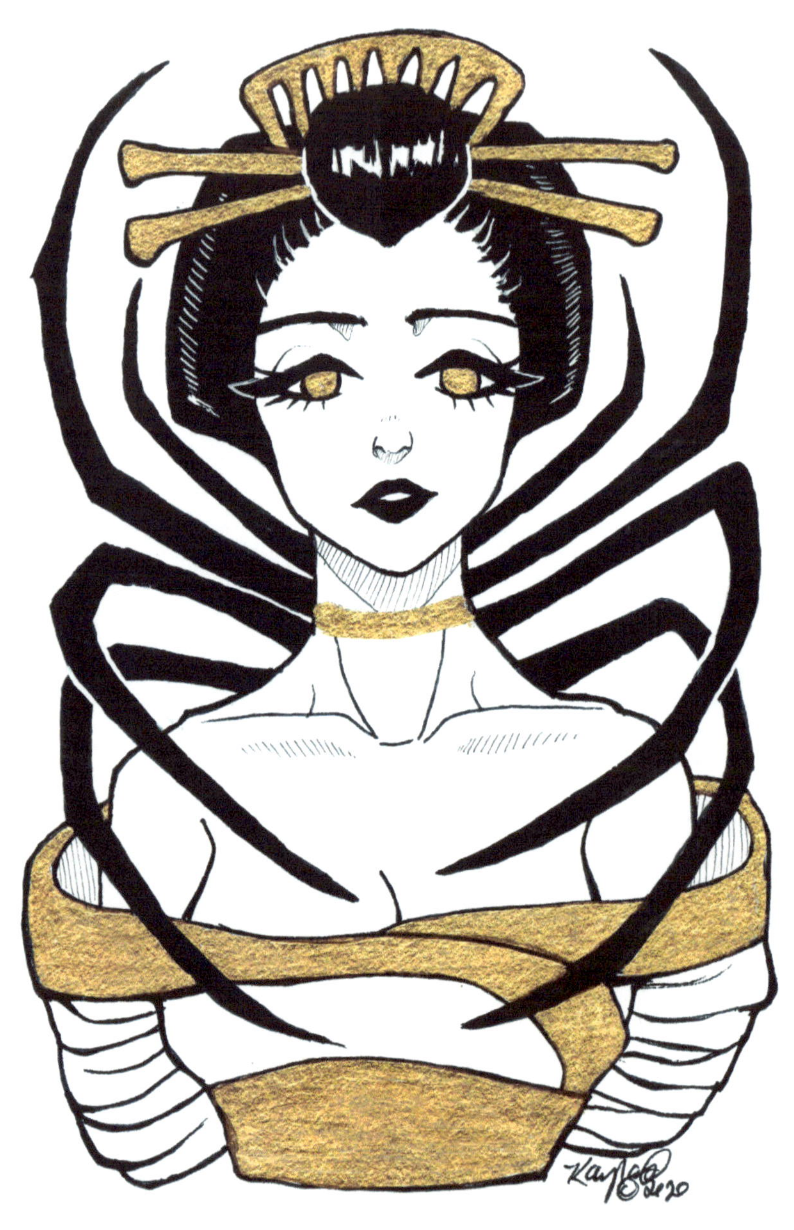

DAY 24 - JOROGUMO

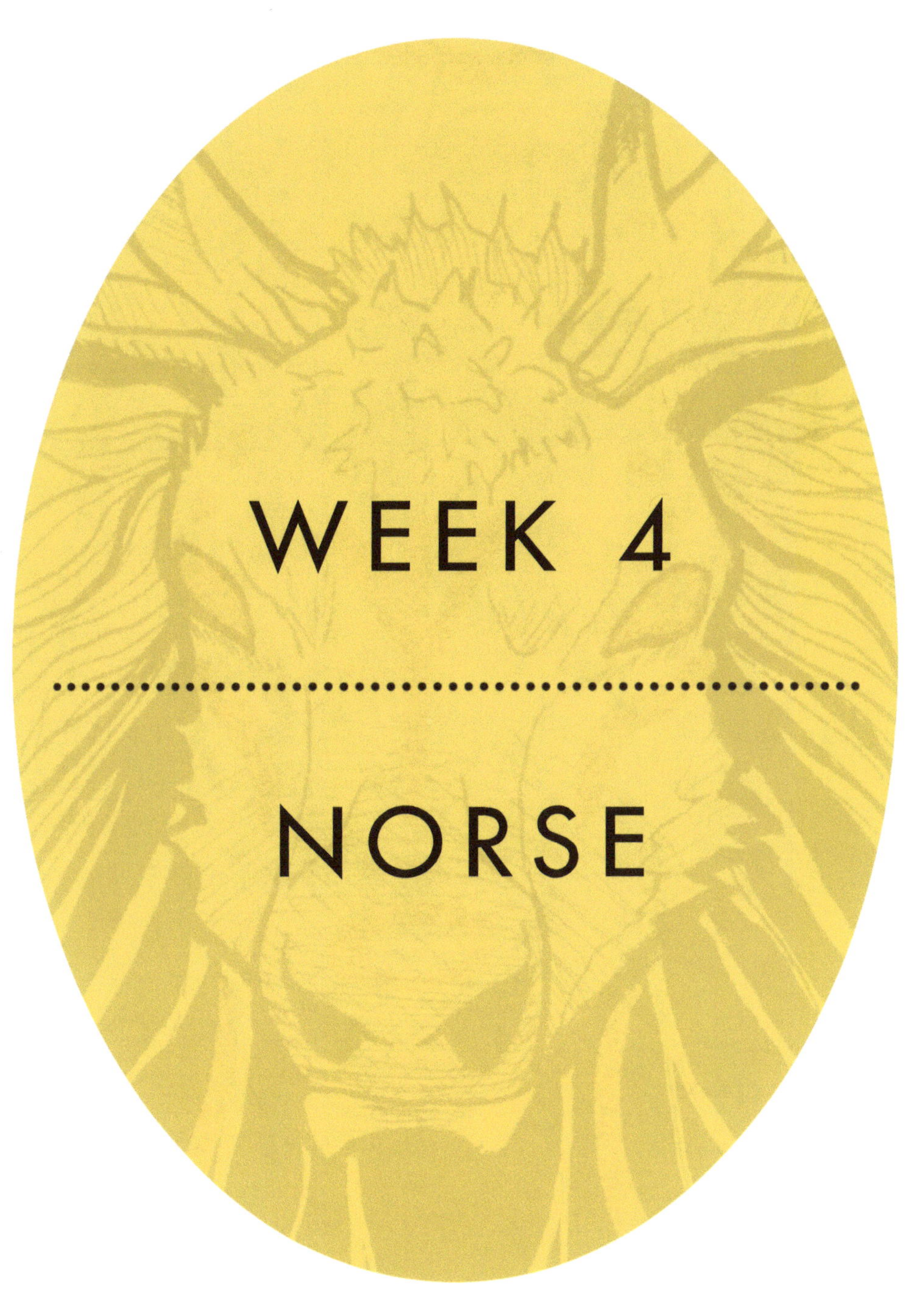
WEEK 4
NORSE

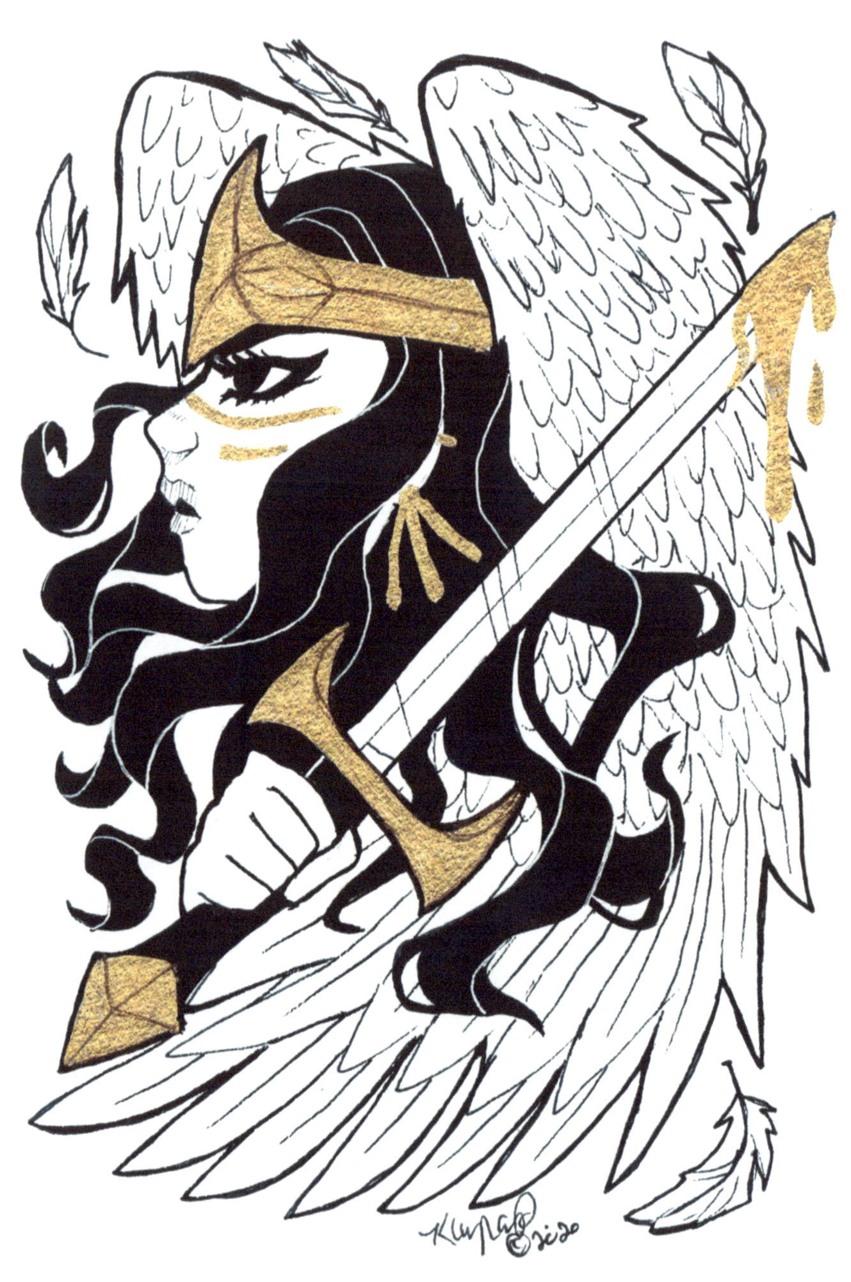

DAY 25 - VALKYRIE

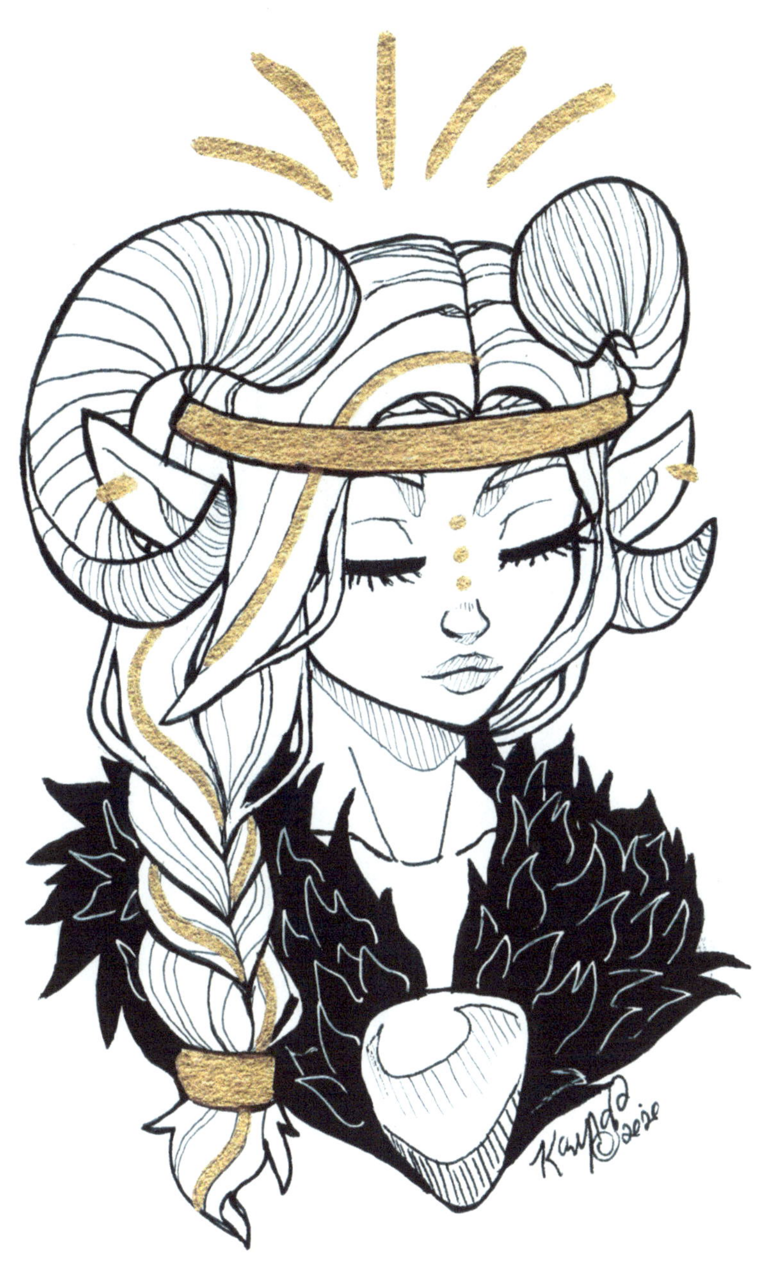

DAY 26 - HEIDRUN

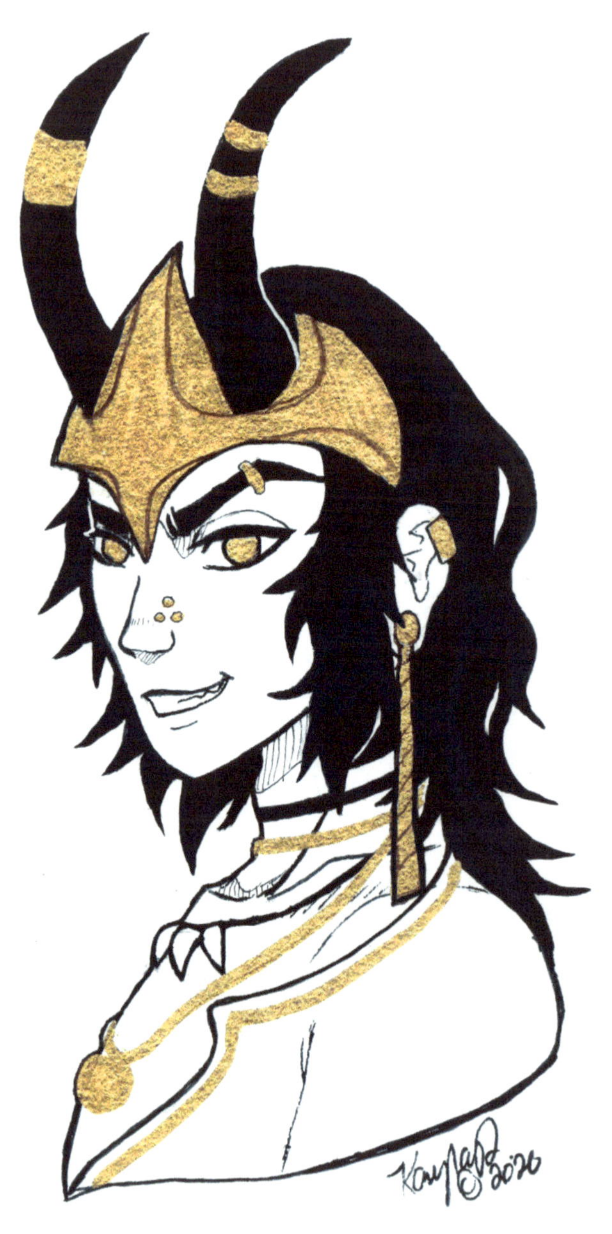

DAY 27 - LOKI

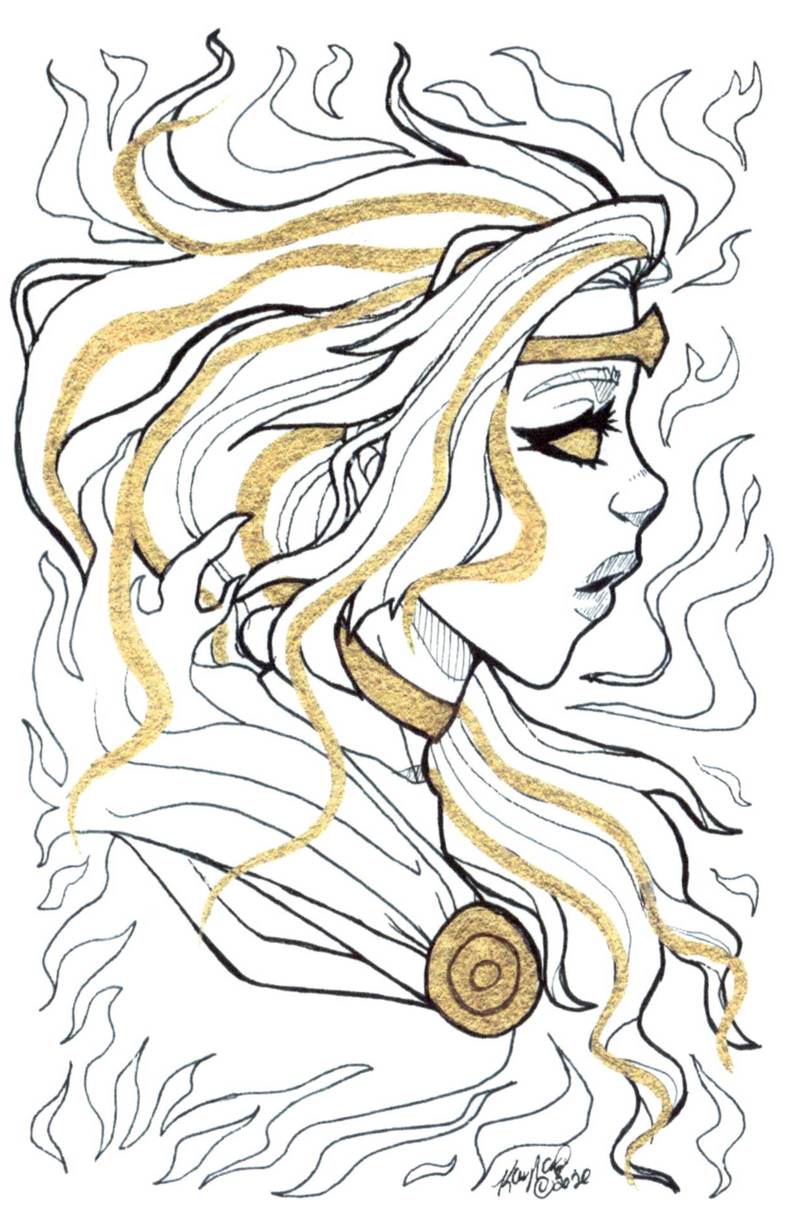

DAY 28 - VORDR

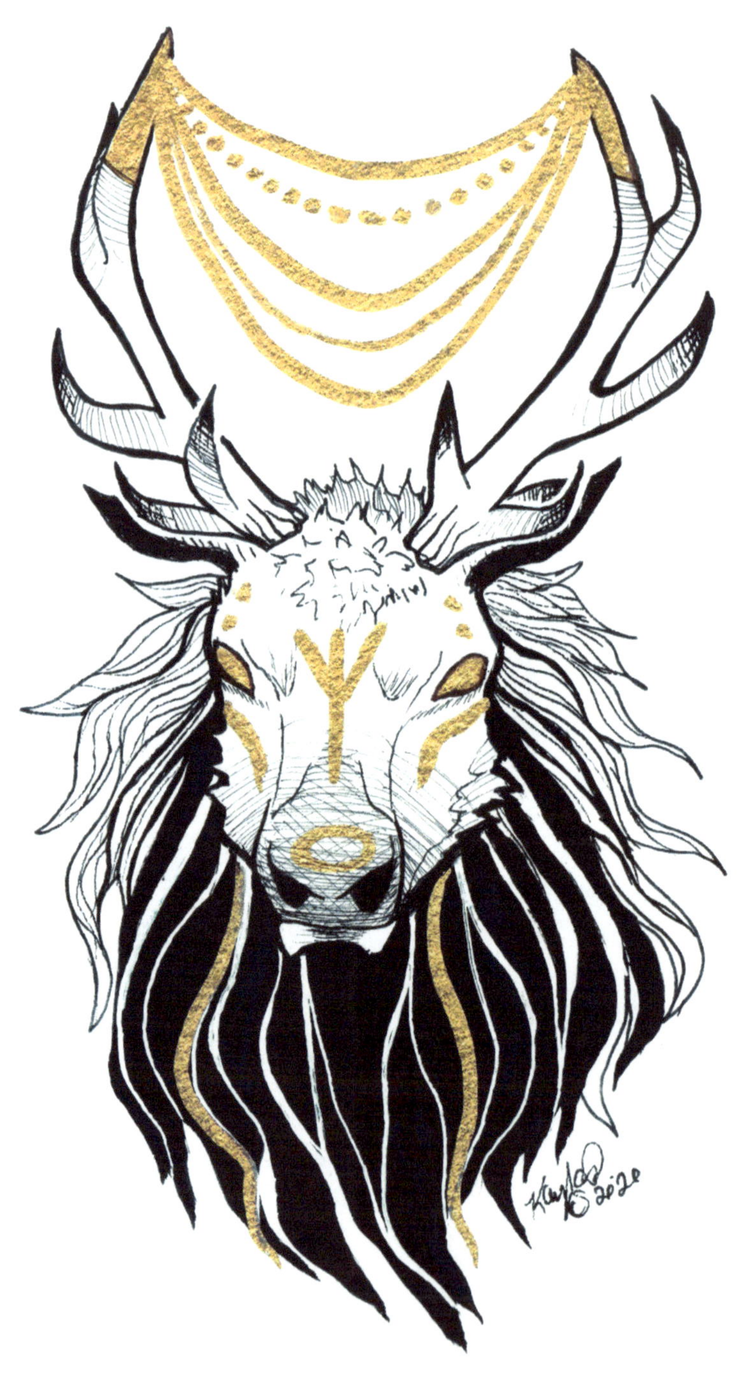

DAY 29 - EIKTHYRNIR

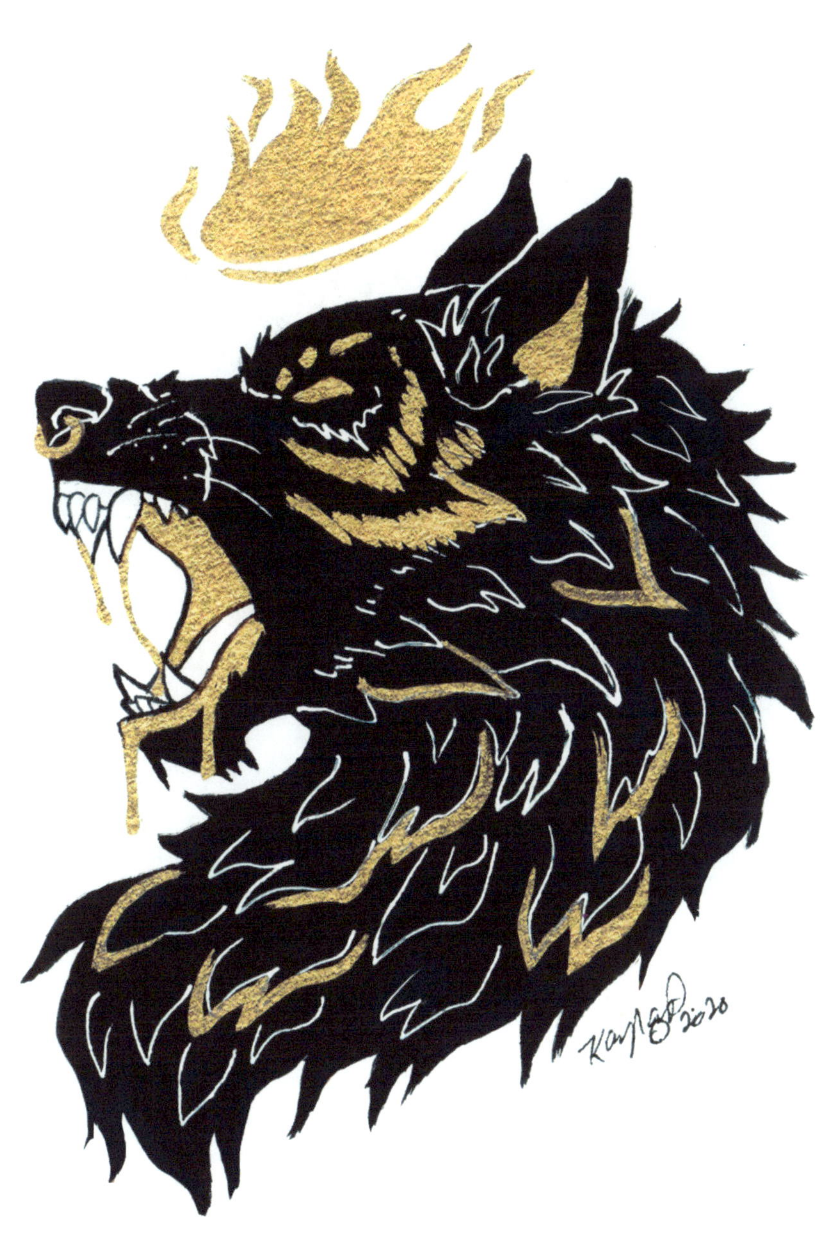

DAY 30 - FENRIR

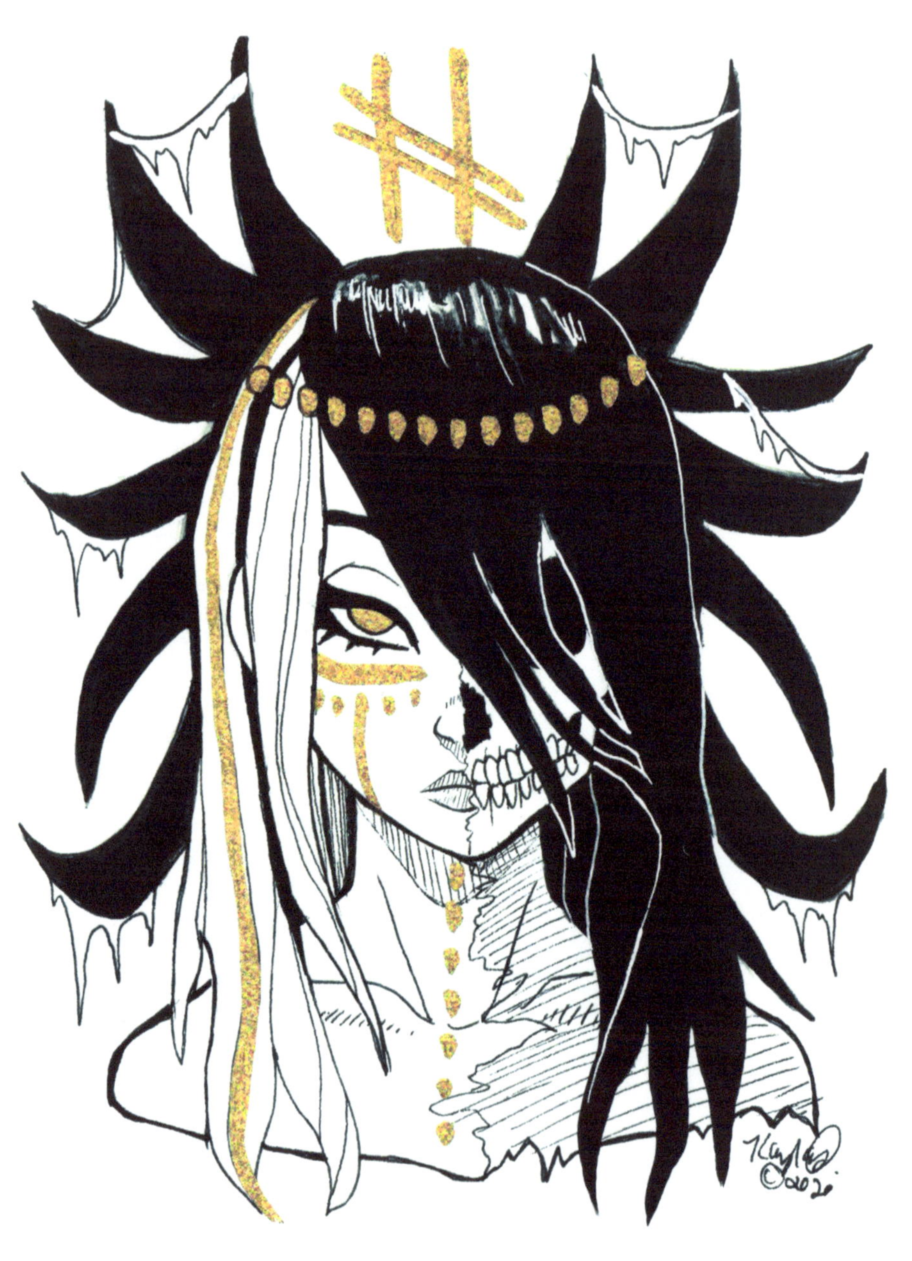

DAY 31 - HEL

THE ARTIST

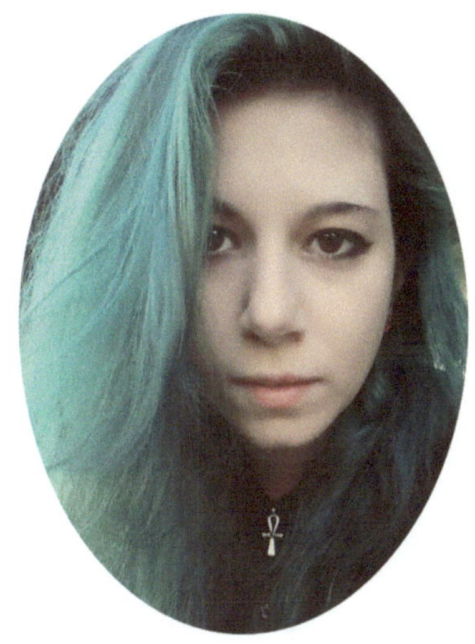

Hi! My name is Kayla Speciale. I am from Pittsburgh, PA and I am a graduate of the Art Institute of Pittsburgh, majoring in graphic design. But, apart from graphic design, I love illustration. My favorite illustration style to work with is digital art but I occassionally do pen and ink as well. Art isn't my only passion, however. I love to read and write stories, novels and comics/graphic novels particularly in fiction, teen fiction and sci-fi/fantasy. I also love anime, manga art, cosplay, video games and music.

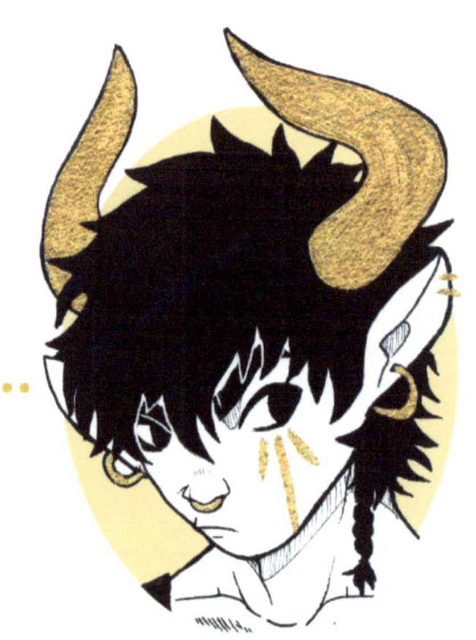